Acknowledgments

After many requests from students, close friends, and my wife, to complete "Tricks of the Grade," I can't express the relief of finishing this book. I also can't express enough appreciation to those who believed what I had to say was worth sharing with others.

What started out as one desperate student's attempt to escape the ghettos of Miami, turned into a blessing that has touched the lives of thousands of students across the country. Although it took over six years to write this book, I definitely believe it was worth the wait. God would never allow this dream to die in my heart, and now I'm able to share it with you.

Thanks to all of you who made *"Tricks of the Grades"* possible, especially my colleague and dear friend Marcia Cross for helping me edit the book. I know you're tired of hearing me say this, but I owe you one.

And thank you (the reader) for purchasing it. I pray that this book helps you as much, if not more, than it has helped me. Live purposefully, and God bless.

This book is dedicated to the many students I have the privilege and pleasure of serving every day as a professor. This book is also dedicated to my loving wife, Felina "Sunshine" Martin, who's heard me "preach" these principles until I was speechless. Sunshine, I can finally say, "read the book."

Tricks of the Grade

...Street-Smart Strategies for Acing College!

Joe Martin Jr.

Published by
RealWorld University Publishing
Tallahassee, FL

Text editing by Marcia Cross

Printed in the USA by

MORRIS PUBLISHING

3212 East Highway 30 • Kearney, NE 68847 • 1-800-650-7888

Table of Contents

Introduction

The Magic Pill

If there was a "magic pill" that could guarantee you straight A's in college, how much would you be willing to pay for it? I guess before you can make an informed decision, you probably would need more information about the "magic pill."

Well, this "pill" has been federally approved by the Food and Drug Administration. The pill also comes with a 100% _double_ your money back guarantee. So there is absolutely no risk involved. There are no side effects. This pill is non-addictive and it's legal! A one bottle supply would be all you will ever need to succeed academically in college. However, since this pill is in very high demand, and there's only a limited supply, it can only go to the highest bidder.

Given these facts, how much would you be willing to pay now? Think about it. You could go to any college in the United States and graduate at the top of your class. You would earn the respect of your peers as well as potential employers. Your parents and/or friends would be proud of you. You would set yourself apart from the rest of your peers. You could get a bachelor's, master's, or even a doctorate degree with ease. You tell me, what could "straight A's" in college do for you?

Again, how much would you be willing to pay for this supply of "magic pills," $10, $100, $1,000, or maybe even more? Oh, by the way, did I mention that financing is available? I'm talking about credit cards, checks, or even IOU's. Well, whatever the amount you would be willing to pay, I want you to keep it pictured in your mind's eye for just a second.

Meet the Professor

My name is Joe Martin, and I'm a professor at Florida A&M University in Tallahassee, Florida. I'm also a national speaker and educational consultant. I want you to know that I've conducted this little test with thousands of students (even my own classes) over the past few years, and the highest bid I ever received was $25,000! Now that may sound a little ridiculous to you, but that student (a college student) insisted that if she attended Harvard University and graduated with a 4.0 GPA in medicine or law, her $25,000 investment in that "pill" would be well worth it. Looking at the history of Harvard graduates who have graduated in the top 5% of their class, it would be difficult to refute her logic. Considering the endless possibilities, a $25,000 bid may even be a little on the low side.

Let's look at it another way. How much are you (or your parents) paying for your college education now? Is it more than $25,000? Now let me ask you this, did the college offer you any guarantees? I didn't think so.

Regardless, I have some good news and some bad news concerning this "magic pill." And to make it quick and painless, I'll start with the bad news first. The bad news is that there is no such pill that will guarantee a student straight A's in college. If there was, that person would be very rich and famous. But I'm sure it's safe to assume that you already knew that.

However, I do have some good news. Although there is no such "magic pill," there is an untapped resource for securing excellent grades in college, and that resource is "YOU!"

Believe it or not, the solution to graduating at the top or near the top of your academic class lies within you like a sleeping giant. This book will help you pull out that wealth of knowledge and awaken that giant. After applying these strategies and "tricks," you will start achieving grades even your friends won't even believe.

You don't believe me? **Well if you apply <u>ALL</u> of the strategies I'm about to teach you, and you're unsatisfied with the results you see within the first semester, I will give you your money back for the book, no questions asked.** All you would have to do is provide me a copy of your college transcript to verify any grade you've received less than a "B." **"Tricks of** the Grade" is **GUARANTEED**. However, these "tricks of the grade" will only work if you work. Matter of fact, when I give my LIVE seminars, I offer students a $100 for each course in which they receive less than a "B" after applying <u>ALL</u> of my strategies. In six years of teaching the "tricks," I am proud to say, **not one student has ever called to even complain or claim a refund.** They (the tricks) work!

So how can I be so confident about these techniques, even to a point of cockiness? Well, I believe I have four valid reasons:

1. I've tried each and every one of these techniques myself as a college student, and guess what, they work!
2. I've taught thousands of college students across the country these same techniques, and guess what, they work!
3. These techniques are different than any other techniques you'll ever read, hear, or try, and guess what, they work!
4. I'm a now professor myself, and guess what, I know they work!

From High School to Manhood

Before we dive into the "Tricks of the Grade," I think it's important for you to know why and how I developed these "tricks." I wish I could claim pure genius, but I'm afraid I might get hit by a bolt of lightening. The truth of the matter is that most (not all) of tricks of grade came out of desperation rather than inspiration. When I say desperate, I mean desperate. I didn't want to make the same mistakes in college that I did during my high school years. Let me explain.

For many teenagers, the high school years were pretty good times. Personally, I couldn't complain. I was like most high school students, well-liked, involved in athletics and other activities. And like most of my high school friends, I was barely passing my classes. I was what most teachers would describe today as a "C-your-way-through-school" student. That means that I received "C's" in almost everything. Sometimes I believe the only reason I got an "A" in P.E. (physical education) was because our coaches graded on a curve. In spite of this, high school life was still good.

On graduation day, my family and I were ecstatic. I had grown up in one of the toughest inner-city ghettoes in Miami, Florida, and graduating from high school meant beating the odds. Matter of fact, I was the only high school senior out of approximately 25 or so in my neighborhood that year who was graduating "on time."

We were very poor, and although we didn't have much, we always seemed to have just enough to get by. My mother, sister, aunt, and godmother comprised my family unit. Only one had graduated from high school at the time, and none had ever completed college. So graduation day was a monumental moment for me as well as my family.

I can remember that day as if it were yesterday; my family was proud, my friends were proud, my neighborhood was proud, and even people I didn't know were proud of me. Ironically though, everyone was proud of me, except me. My high school graduation day, although memorable, had been one of the worst days of my life.

Initially it started out great, until I got a dose of reality during the graduation ceremony.

I was graduating with a 2.2 cumulative GPA in a senior class of approximately 550 students. Like I said before, I was "C-ing my way through school." The atmosphere in the Miami Convention Center was incredible. People were cheering for their family and friends, and the flow of the program was moving swiftly. A friend of mine was sitting next to me at the time, and he was taking in the energy of the evening. As we were sitting and listening to the announcer call out the names of the senior class, something caught my eye. I spotted a group of students sitting in the front row of our graduating class.

I asked my friend, who was sitting next to me, "Who are those people in the front row with those gold 'things' draped around their necks?" He replied, "Oh Joe, they're the Top 50."

And in my ignorance I responded, "The Top 50 what?" "Those students in the front row are the top 50 graduates in our high school," he said. He continued, "They're the smartest students in our school."

Although I was considered only an "average" student, I had always been happy with my academic performance in school, until I realized that there were no African Americans in that group of 50.

And even though our school did not have a large percentage of African Americans (maybe 25%), I felt we had enough to have at least one student represented out of 50. As an African American student, I felt both embarrassed and ashamed. I was embarrassed for my family because I wasn't in that top 50, and I was ashamed of myself and my race because I didn't even try.

I couldn't speak for anyone else, but I felt that I belonged in that Top 50. Although my grades did not reflect that I was an exceptional student, no one could have convinced me that I wasn't capable. I felt that I was just as smart as anyone else in my graduating class. I finally had to accept that disgraceful fact that almost every student hears at least one time or another during grade school, "I just didn't 'apply' myself." And there was no one to blame, but me.

My mother and family could not understand why my attitude had changed so dramatically that night in just a couple of hours, but I understood perfectly. Anyone who has an ounce of self-respect, especially as much pride as I thought I had, cannot sit around and settle for second best.

Unfortunately, it took until that moment to realize that my forefathers had paid the price and sacrificed their lives for me to get an opportunity for an education; and my thanks to them was settling for mediocrity. I couldn't live with that; I was disgusted.

Surprisingly, I discovered that the only difference between me sitting in the crowd of 500 and those sitting in the crowd of 50 was **not a matter of my I.Q., but rather a lack of my <u>I Will</u>**. That same night, I promised my mother and myself that "I would" no longer settle for just being "average." As you will find out as you go through "Tricks of the Grade," average just means you're better than the worst, because in actuality, you're worst than the best. I hope that makes sense; if not, it will later.

Thus, these techniques, these so-called "tricks of the grade," are the results of one college student who was fed up with mediocrity. These strategies were the result of a college student who became desperate enough to start rebuilding his pride and self-respect.

I took these techniques and transformed a 2.2 high school GPA into a 3.8 college GPA. I took these same techniques and moved from the middle of the class in high school to the top of my college class in my major. I took these same techniques and went from one of many students to "Student of the Year" in my major. I took these same techniques and went from low SAT scores to being the youngest tenure-earning faculty member ever hired to teach in the Florida State University System.

Through the successful completion of my bachelor's and master's degrees, I never received a grade less than a B.   Do they work? You better believe they do, and I'm going to show you **exactly** how I did it?

But Will It Work For Me?

Although these techniques worked for me, you may be wondering if they'll work for you. Yes they will! Originally, I didn't think they would work for others, until I started sharing them with my family members and my students. Through their constant urging, I am writing this book.

It doesn't matter what kind of student you are. If you're an "average" to "below average" student, your grades will improve dramatically -- if you apply my strategies. If you're already a good student, these techniques will help you maintain or "pad" your current GPA and save you a lot of time. Is it that easy? Quite frankly, no! But is it possible? Emphatically, yes! In order to apply my "tricks of the grade" techniques, you will need to possess the following personal characteristics:

1. **Courage** -- a willingness to step out of your comfort zone.
2. **Commitment** -- a whatever it takes kind of attitude.
3. **Common Sense** -- an ability to master the obvious.

If you do not have these three basic necessities, close the book right now and send it back for a full refund. The three traits mentioned above are the cornerstones of most, if not all, of the techniques. Testimonials from students who have successfully applied my strategies reveal that <u>fear, laziness,</u> and <u>YOU</u> are the only obstacles in your way. I'll give you the academic common sense you need, but you'll have to supply the commitment and the courage on your own.

So before you waste any of your valuable time and energy in reading this book, <u>HONESTLY</u> answer the following three questions:

1. Do I really want to become more successful in college?
2. Am I willing to follow these techniques to the letter?
3. Do I believe I deserve and can achieve better grades?

If you answered "yes" to all three, we can begin. If you answered "no" to any one of them, please stop reading and get your money back for this book.

The Three Truths

Courage, common sense, and commitment are the tools that you must possess in order to make "Tricks of the Grade" work for you. However, there are three truths that you must also keep in mind as you apply each of the strategies. Although these truths sound simple, most college students do not recognize them as being important. Once you accept these truths as fact, I guarantee your road to academic success will be much smoother and more prosperous. So what are they?

Truth #1:   Teachers are human beings, too.

I know this sounds simplistic, but from what I've seen as both a student and college professor, students don't believe this. Because of the professors' degrees and numerous books they've authored, students tend to place their professors on a pedestal; and in some respect, students treat them like they're some kind of god (or least some professors think they are). As human beings, professors have egos like you and me, and teaching gives them a sense of perceived power. And in their own eyes, they are powerful.

A professor's perceived power clouds a student's ability to look at them objectively. So what if we know more than you, does that make us any better than you? No, it just makes us more educated. Students fail to realize that professors are just like them. They have personal lives with personal problems and issues. How do I know? Because I'm one of them (and I knew this fact as a student). Professors have relationship problems, they run numerous errands, pay bills, live on a budget, get sick, run out of toilet paper, get speeding tickets, argue with their employers, etc.

Why do I say all of this? Because one of the biggest mistakes students make is to think that professors are fair. Hello! We're not. We try to be, but we can't be. It's part of human nature. If humans were fair, then we would all spend our money equally at restaurants, gas stations, grocery stores, etc. It's not that we're intentionally trying to be unfair, but we "prefer" certain places, things, *and people* in comparison to others.

Therefore, we (professors) play favorites. I know that most of my colleagues wouldn't want me to tell you this, but it's the truth. You play favorites, I play favorites, so why wouldn't professors do it? There is no one on God's green earth who is totally objective. This is an important concept, because universities and colleges have been preaching objectivity since the dawn of time. That's just not the case. Again, we try to be fair, but it is close to impossible to be totally objective when it comes to students. Even when I became a professor, I tried to dispel this theory and I couldn't do it. Human nature tells us that there will always be certain people we like more than others. This truth leads us to the second truth.

Truth #2:   Your grades aren't everything, but your reputation is.

This is one of the most important facts students fail to recognize. So many times, students are so involved and concerned about their grades, they fail to consider how they're being perceived. Understand this from a professor's point of view, there is a huge difference between an "A" student who is a jerk, and a "B" student who works hard and has earned the respect of her peers. Because of that difference in perception, that "B" student will invariably find the doors of opportunity opened to her more often than that "A" student will. It's called "the way it is."

I tell my students that if you want to succeed on any college or university campus, all you have to do is look at what most of the students are doing, and then do the total opposite. Because if you do what most students do, you're going to get what most students get: frustration, confusion, resentment, mediocrity, etc.

Most students spend too much time worrying about their grades than working on their reputation. Unfortunately, perception is reality, and how you're perceived by your professors will "unfairly" dictate your success as a student.

To give you an example of what I'm talking about, I would like you to participate HONESTLY in the following exercise. I want you to close your eyes right now, and think about the WORST teacher you ever had in either college or high school. Now think of three adjectives that teacher would use to describe your work habits to another teacher, and write your answers in the space provided:

1. _____

2. _____

3. _____

Do these adjectives paint an accurate picture of you? Whether it does or doesn't isn't the point. The truth is, this is how you're perceived in that particular teacher's eyes. We've all heard the phrase that perception is reality; well, it's also true in college.

Now ask yourself, if your next teacher was given this description of you on the first day of class before meeting you, would it have any impact on your reputation? Do you think that professor would form any biases toward you because of that description? You better believe it. Remember when I said that teachers are human beings too? Guess what, they also gossip like students do.

Believe it or not, professors spend more time talking about you than you do about them. Remember, this is our job, not yours. This was one of the few theories I could not prove until I became a professor.

The sad part is that it may take you <u>four years</u> to build a good college student reputation, but all it takes is <u>one</u> professor to ruin it. Another little known fact is that the smaller the school or class size, the more important your reputation is.

I repeat, your grades aren't everything, but your reputation is! Think about it for a second, do you think that a student who is known in the math department as responsible, hard working, and focused, has an advantage over one who is known as irresponsible, lazy, and confused? You better believe it. It's your job to set yourself apart from other students *(see the section Student Stranglers)*. Accept this truth, and you'll be on your way to academic success!

Truth #3: There's no easy way, just a better way.

You probably purchased this book because you thought it would make your college experience a lot easier. Well, it won't. However, I do believe it will make your experience a lot better. Your mother or father probably told you that anything worth having is worth working hard for. This is true. These "tricks" are not a "get rich quick" approach to a successful academic career. They take time and effort, and they will work, if you do.

For the record, let me dispel any "pie in the sky" ideas you may have about my strategies. You will have to attend class, you will have to take notes, you will have to study, and you will have to work hard. "WHAT" you have to do to succeed in college hasn't changed, but "HOW" you do it is an entirely different story. My "HOW" strategies will show you how to succeed academically in ways that will sometimes shock you. These "tricks" are simple, but they are not easy. You will find out quickly, what's often nothing more than common sense, isn't always common knowledge. Remember what I told you earlier. You need courage, common sense, and commitment. And the only obstacles in your way are fear, laziness, and YOU!

The "Tricks of the Grade" is broken down into three parts: Base Building Basics, Teacher Taming Techniques, and Street-Smart Study Strategies. There are a total of ten (10) "tricks." Believe it or not, most students won't even make it through the first three. Why? I don't know, that's just human nature I guess. That's why it's so important to do the opposite of what most people (especially students) would do, and you will be successful.

So tie your shoe laces, and let's get started with the "Tricks of the Grade." These are strategies that will change your academic career forever.

Part I: Base Building Basics

Now I'm no architect or construction worker, but everyone knows that a house is only as strong as the foundation it is built upon. We know that a house built on sand will surely fall, so to avoid that fate, we will seek to build our "Tricks of the Grade" home on cement. Therefore, I call this section the "Base Building Basics" because they're the foundation of "Tricks of the Grade."

Without these three basics, the rest of strategies would be rendered useless. Matter of fact, I will venture to say that if you internalize and solidify these three basics in your thinking, you probably won't need the others.

I know that sounds ridiculous, but that's why students have had so much success with this system. College is not about aptitude, it's about attitude, and these three base builders will help you adopt a winning one. The reason I've never had a student unsatisfied with these tricks is because once they've whipped their attitude into shape, they found that they didn't need ALL of the other tricks to succeed. Just call this the inside-out approach to success in college. That's what makes this system so different. These strategies focus on the person, not your performance.

Enough already, let's start with the first one. . .

Chapter 1: Why Ask Why?

The first step to achieving academic success in college is to establish a red hot "Why Statement" for yourself.

I intentionally listed this strategy first because I believe it's the most important strategy in this entire book. Sure, the other strategies will get you excited and hyped about applying them in class, but without this element, the first sign of danger or trouble in college will send you running for cover.

Let me start by asking you a question. When you first applied to the college, what kind of information did your admissions application request? Other than your name, social security number and mailing address, the application probably asked you for your SAT/ACT scores, previous classes taken, overall grade point average, maybe extracurricular activities, your proposed major, and some other irrelevant junk.

I'm sorry for calling it junk, but I believe we could save the world a lot of trees if colleges asked students what I believe is the most important question before entering college: **Why do you want to go to college?** Think about it, if you had the highest grade point average in your high school class, perfect standardized test scores, and you were voted most likely to succeed, but the only reason you were going to college was to get away from your parents, do you really think you would perform at your peak in college? Even if you did, you'd be miserable trying.

College is not difficult, but it's not a piece a cake either. You have professors (present company included) who have tough course requirements which they expect every student to meet. If you are not focused on your purpose for being in that classroom, procrastination and frustration will begin to set in. Before you know it, college will swallow you up before you know what happened.

If I was the president of a university, other than your name and social security number, I would only ask you one question on the application: **Why do you want to go to college?** Read that question again; I didn't ask why my college or university, but why any college or university. I would base your admission to my college on the quality of your response to that question. Why, you ask? Because if you show me a student who is excelling in college, I will show you a student who has a red hot desire to graduate.

Just think about it for a second. Have you ever wondered how certain students even got into college in the first place? They don't show up for class, they don't study, they don't turn in their assignments, and the list goes on and on. Now understand, these are not bad students; they managed to get out of high school, didn't they? They just lack a strong purpose for being in college. Some of these students figure it out later and, unfortunately, some never do.

The Non-Traditional Approach

Don't take my word for it, just look around in your next class. If your college is anything like the ones in which I've attended and taught, you will find a handful of what colleges call "nontraditional students." And if you don't know, a non-traditional (NT) student is a student who is older than most of the students at the college. I've met some NTs as young as 30-something and as old as 60-something.

Have you ever noticed when an NT is in your class he or she seems somewhat nervous. And when you think about it, could you really blame them? They're sitting in a classroom filled with students half their age, some young enough to be their children. Do you think that could make someone feel a little self-conscious? Of course it could. These type of students have been out of school, on average, about 10 or more years. A personal NT friend of mine had been out of school for over 40 years before she decided to attend college! No joke.

Well, on the first day of classes, you've probably noticed that

NTs are not shy when it comes to standing up in class and introducing themselves. They are usually quick to tell you their age and how long they've been out of school. The scenario goes a little something like this.

"Hello, my name is Jane Doe. I'm from Miami, Florida, and I'm 42 years old. I've been out of school for over 20 years, and now I'm back in college majoring in accounting. I have two sons, one has already graduated from college, and the other is a senior in high school. Although I'm a little nervous, I'm really excited about being back in school. I just hope I do well."

We're all familiar with this routine.

I don't know about you, but every time that scenario took place in class, my heart just went out to those NTs. Think about it, they haven't had algebra and chemistry in over a decade, and we know friends who just had those classes last semester and still failed. So it's normal to think that these NTs don't have a chance; or do they? Yeah, that's what we think until the end of the semester or graduation day rolls around. Have you ever noticed that those NTs usually end up receiving the best grades in the class, and they also manage to graduate with honors.

Now you may call it a coincidence, but not me. Because after I saw my 60-something friend get the top grades in our class, I didn't hesitate to ask her about it. I would encourage you do the same. Instead of marveling at how "old" they are, talk to NTs and see what makes them tick. You will be amazed. My NT friend didn't give me any mind blowing study strategies; matter of fact, she wasn't even aware that there was such a thing called "study strategies."

So I asked her a question that had burned on my mind since the first day I saw her, **"Why are you in college?"** Her answer astounded me, thus the reason why this is the first trick of the grade. She said that when she was in her early twenties, she was married to a man who did not believe that a woman should go to college. Therefore, he made her stay at home and raise the family, even though she wanted to pursue an education. Not only that, he didn't even want her reading educational books in their home. In her own words, "He was a very controlling man."

Unlike today's society in which divorces are requested if your mate sneezes too loud, she refused to ask him for a divorce. She continued to raise her four daughters while he continued to work his blue-collar job. All the while, she longed to pursue her dream of becoming a writer (her major was communication).

As fate would have it, after her children moved away from home, her husband became ill and eventually died. Although under his control for over 40 years, she still loved him and missed him. She found herself alone with only his memory and a fading dream of becoming a writer. But instead of feeling sorry for herself, she decided to take control of her own destiny and pursue her passion for writing. She applied for admission and was accepted, and the rest is, as they say it, is history. By the way, she ended up graduating with honors.

This is what I mean when I say that school is not about aptitude, but attitude. This woman didn't even have SAT/ACT scores, but she achieved a higher grade point average than 90% of her peers. I'm sure she, if you asked her, would attribute her academic success to having a strong WHY. I've asked other NTs during my years of studying and teaching about their "whys" for college, and I've received some of the following responses:

"I've hit the glass ceiling on my job, and I need a degree to get promoted."
"My spouse died, and the money he left won't be enough to support me and the kids."
"I've always wanted to become a teacher, but I got pregnant when I was in school and dropped out."
"I have a little boy, and I want to provide a better life for him than I had."
"My boss told me that I've maxed out my pay potential, and a degree will allow me to make more money."

"Someday I want my children to get a college degree, and I don't want them to ask me why I didn't get mine."

Now, ask yourself, how do the above responses compare to the ones we've heard before from our younger classmates:

"Man, my mother made me go."
"My dad said that it was either this or get a job."
"I couldn't think of anything else better to do, so I decided to try the college thing."
"I wanted to be with my friends so we could pledge together."
"I'm here so I can figure out what I want to do with my life."
"Man, I'm here to meet the babes."

Do you see the difference? If you have a weak "WHY," college will only become a nuisance and a four-year pain in the neck for you. The entire four years you're in school you'll be asking the same nagging question, "Why am I putting myself through this?" And if you don't think the college ordeal is worth it, you'll either quit or become a career student (you know, the 7-year plan to get a four-year degree).

But if you establish a strong "WHY," you'll have the energy to put up with the crap in order to graduate. Your WHY gives you a reason to keep going even when the going gets tough. I know because I've been there many times. See, you have to understand, there is no right or wrong WHY, just a strong or weak one. Look again at the examples above; technically, there's nothing wrong with any of those responses (maybe the babe one), the first group is just stronger than the second group. Because of that, the second group will always have a tougher road academically.

The Shot in the Arm

Allow me to give you a personal example from my college days. I mentioned earlier that I grew up in one of the toughest ghettos in Miami, Florida. Since I went away to school, like most students, I called home quite frequently to keep in touch with my family.

Since my finances (and my mom's) were limited, I could only afford to talk to my mother about once every two weeks. I'd talk to her on the telephone usually on a Wednesday. Every week we talked I could hear gun shots and sirens in the background. Since I had been away from home so long, these noises caught me by surprise. I'd ask my mother, "What's that noise in the background?" She would calmly respond, "Oh baby, they're just shooting." She would say it so casual that I thought I was in an episode of the Twilight Zone.

Why do I tell you this, because if you'd ask me when I was in college, **"Why was I in college,"** I would have told you, "to move my mother and younger sister out of the ghetto." That's not a right or wrong WHY, but it sure was a strong one for me.

While my friends complained about our classes and our teachers, I was focused on one thing and one thing only, graduate and move Mama and Penny out of there. My WHY was so compelling that I couldn't help but succeed. My WHY was bigger than any obstacle, teacher, course or circumstance that was in my way. My WHY helped me to overcome racist professors, boring professors, irrelevant courses, difficult courses, personal problems, financial problems, you name it. My classmates marveled at my motivation, but if the truth be told, it was more of my desperation that helped me to graduate with honors. My WHY told me that I only had one chance to make this opportunity count, and I wasn't going to blow it.

So the first step in "Tricks of Grade" is to establish a strong WHY that will help you weather the storms and turbulent waters of academia. Ask yourself, **"Why are you in college anyway?"** If you can't come up with something compelling, something that burns inside you, something that's bigger than your problems, you will find yourself in the sea of mediocrity hoping someone saves you before you drown. The only alternative would be to quit college and return when you've found a strong enough reason to attend. So write down your WHY statement today (length doesn't matter), and make sure it's in a place you can read it every day of your college career.

Quick Trick Action Steps: Why Ask Why?

1. Establish a strong, compelling, personal "WHY" for being in college.
2. Write or type out your "WHY STATEMENT."
3. Test that why statement by asking yourself these three questions:

   a.) Am I willing to do **whatever it takes** to make this a reality?
   b.) Am I willing to **pay the price with blood, sweat, and tears** to graduate?
   c.) Am I willing to **take the garbage** that comes along with the college experience?

4. Ask yourself, did I answer the previous three questions honestly and blamelessly? (If no, find another "why.")
5. Put your why statement in a place where you can read it at least once a week (preferably Mondays).

Now that you've established your WHY for college, you must transition to the next step...

Chapter 2: Determine Your Destination

The second step to achieving academic success in college is to determine what you want to achieve during your years in college.

You've already established your reasons for even starting this four-year journey down the road of academia, now you must determine what you want to achieve along the way. I call this step *"Determining Your Destination."*

If you ask the average college student, **"What do you want to achieve while you're in college?** They'll usually tell you things like, "graduate, get a job, finish on time, etc." Now you may ask, what's wrong with that? Well nothing's wrong with that if you like underdeveloped pictures. See, most students start college with little or no direction. They're unclear about what they want. Some even want others to tell them what they should want. If you don't know exactly where you want to go, any road will get you there.

If you planned a spring break trip to an unfamiliar place, do you also plan to be lost and confused? Certainly not. When taking a trip, you usually map out a course (i.e., directions), look for destination markers (i.e., landmarks, certain interstate signs, city signs), and talk to people who've already been there before. You do this just to make sure you don't get lost. So, why should your college journey be any different? Take the trip by first planning your course.

Not Following the Crowd

Goals are the same as directions to a chosen destination. We're not talking lifetime goals, we're talking about short-term college goals (five years or less). Remember, I told you earlier in the book that the key to success in college is to watch what most students do and then do the total opposite? Let's face it, most don't set goals. Allow me to illustrate this point.

.. nas already been documented, almost to a point of overkill, now important goal setting is to one's success. We ALL know this. You would be hard pressed to shock any college student with the goal setting concept. Given that fact, if you stepped into a typical classroom of 100 students today and asked them *how many of you set goals*, how many of them do you think would raise their hands? Well let me tell what I usually see when I ask this question. I will usually get about 30 students raising their hands and 10 are probably lying (but that's okay).

Of that 30, how many of them would respond if asked, *how many of you have your goals written down?* I usually will get 10 out of 30 students raising their hands (hopefully no liars). Of the 10 remaining, how many of them would respond if asked, *how many of you read them at least once a semester?* After that question, I usually see about five (5) hands still raised (sometimes less).

The goal setting concept has been beat into our heads since we entered high school, but most of us (95%) still don't get it! This is why you, as a college student, can't afford to follow the crowd. It was once said that, "those who don't set goals are bound to work for those who do."

The truth of the matter is that most students are starting their college journey just hoping to arrive at their destination. Why do you think most students act relieved, giddy, and somewhat childish when they eventually graduate (you've seen some of their theatrics on the ceremony stage)? Because most weren't really sure that they would ever graduate (i.e., reach their destination).

My suggestion is to determine your destination before you take the trip so you can enjoy the ride along the way. Haven't you ever noticed that when you drive somewhere, you seem to be a little more comfortable and confident when you have clear directions? This is called a clue. Set yourself up for success by plotting and planning the course before you take it.
I guarantee you won't regret it.

21

Blind Faith

Allow me to share another personal story with you. I started college at the age of 17, and the first thing I did on the night before classes began was determine five (5) goals I wanted to achieve BEFORE graduation. Why only five? Because most goal-setting experts say that anything more than five would become overwhelming. And God knows I didn't need any more stress in my life.

Listed below are the five goals I wrote down that night and a short explanation about each:

1.) Graduate with a least a 3.5 grade point average or better.

Rationale: I told you earlier about my experience in high school and how I never really put forth my best effort (result = 2.2 GPA). I remembered the promise I made to my mother to do my best, and I planned to keep it. Also, I knew that if I accomplished this goal, it would increase my chances of success beyond college. So I figured, why not give it a try.

2.) Join and become actively involved in three student organizations (at least one in my major).

Rationale: I quickly learned from previous graduates that if they could go back to college and do it all over again, most said that they would have become more active on campus. They also believed that "active" students (i.e., those in leadership roles) tended to get better job offers with higher salaries. Hey, who was I to argue? Count me in.

3.) Receive at least two job offers in my major BEFORE I graduate.

Rationale: I'm sure you would agree that most students, upon graduation, are either unemployed, underemployed (working outside of their major), or undecided about what they're going to do next. I didn't want to become another statistic, so I "planned" diligently to put myself in a better situation upon graduation.

4.) Buy my first home immediately upon graduation.

Rationale: Talking to other successful graduates, I found that most were unhappy with their tax/financial situation. For a single person earning $30,000 a year coming right out of college, Uncle Sam is just licking his chops to take most of it from you. I didn't want this happen to me, so I thought it would nice to have a tax shelter when I graduated. Also, I noticed that most students rented when they graduated, so that meant it couldn't be right. I wanted to be different, so I did the opposite.

5.) Save at least $2,000 in cash by graduation day.

Rationale: I just thought it would be nice to have some cash stashed away in savings. That's all.

Given these "wants," you have to understand that I had no clue "how" I would achieve them. But I was certain that if I had a strong enough "WHY" for my "wants," the "HOW" would reveal itself later. This is an important concept to grasp. Many times we fail to set goals for ourselves because we don't know, at the moment of goal conception, how we will achieve them. I'm telling you right now that you don't have to know "how," just know "why." The "how" will reveal itself eventually. I hope that makes sense.

23

Survey Says...

Well, how did things turn out for me? I achieved goal. I graduated with a 3.8 grade point average. Ho it? That's why I wrote this book, to show you "how."

I achieved the second goal. I joined and actively participated in five organizations, and I was president in one and vice president in another, both within my major.

I achieved the third goal. I received three job offers in my major BEFORE I graduated. Of course I could only accept one, which ended up being the worst of the three (but that story is for another book).

I achieved the fourth. I was blessed to be able to purchase my first home when I graduated. How did I do it? Careful planning, good credit, and a lot of praying. For details on any of these goals, write or e-mail me (noexqse@aol.com). I would love to share it with you.

However, I didn't achieve the fifth goal. I fell short. In retrospect, I wonder if it had anything to do with me having a weak "why" for it in the first place. Hmm?, something to think about. When I speak across the country to college students, some tell me that the reason they don't set goals is because of what happened to me. They say, "Joe, you pursued those five goals for three and a half years only to fall one short." Is that the craziest thing you've ever heard or what? Honestly, this is what I hear from students.

Now understand, whenever you set a goal (destination) for yourself, you are indeed setting yourself up for failure. There is a 50/50 chance you will either succeed or fail. But my question is this, what are your chances if you don't set a goal? That's right, you have a 0% chance of succeeding! I don't know about you, but if someone gave me 50% odds on winning the lotto, I'd be the first one in line buying a ticket. That's why you need to give yourself at least half of a chance to succeed. Start today!

1. Write down five goals you want to achieve BEFORE you graduate from college.
2. Examine each goal and make sure that each is realistic (out of sight, but not out of reach), specific (unclear goals equal unclear results), measurable (so you can check your progress), and has a deadline.
3. Answer the following questions as they pertain to **each one** of the five goals you listed (write out your responses):

> 1.) What will I gain if I achieve this goal?
> 2.) What will it cost me if I don't achieve this goal?
> 3.) Who could help me achieve this goal?
> 4.) What could prevent me from achieving this goal?
> 5.) Who can I get to hold me accountable for my goals (and tell them)?

4. Read your goals at least once a semester (I kept a copy in every notebook that I had).

Now that you've determined your goals along the journey, you must put one more base building block in place...

Chapter 3: Break the Curve

The third step to achieving academic success in college is to expect and believe you will receive the best grade in the class.

This is the last base building strategy, and I believe it will immediately transform your grades. But it's also the toughest one to internalize. "Breaking the Curve" means you must expect to succeed. Why is this such a tough concept to internalize? Because most people have been programmed to think of themselves as being average and to accept mediocrity. I know because I was one of them. Most of us doubt ourselves and our abilities. You don't believe me, try giving one of your friends a sincere compliment, and watch their reaction. If they're like most people, they will be a little embarrassed and even try to deny the compliment.

This third step speaks to the essence of who you are and what you believe about yourself. When I was in high school, my self esteem was below average. I was short (still am), skinny (still am), and often overlooked by females (hit a home run). I really didn't believe that I was an unattractive guy because a lot of my less attractive friends didn't have a problem dating women. However, my level of self confidence was nothing to be desired.

It wasn't until my coach asked me to join the wresting team when my confidence begin to take a turn for the better. My physical confidence somehow spilled over into my emotional confidence. Now don't get me wrong, I still was no lady magnet, but I noticed that as my confidence increased so did female interest. The point of the matter is that I noticed that people believe in those who believe in themselves. It works the same way academically. Professors believe in students who believe in themselves.

As a "C" student, I don't think I really doubted myself, but that's the impression I gave my teachers. And I have a saying, we don't get what we want out of life, we get what we expect.

Nothing demonstrates this point more so than the following illustration:

The Grading System Set-up

A = Excellent
B = Good
C = Average
D = Bad
F = Worst

Listed above is the typical grading scale at a typical college or university. Some colleges have a plus and minus system, but the concept I will illustrate is still the same.

Being totally honest with yourself, have you ever been in a difficult course or had a difficult professor in college in which you said to yourself or to another person, "Man, I hope I pass this class." When I ask this question across the country, almost unanimously students raise their hand in confession (present company included). I did it all the time throughout high school, just hoping I'd pass.

However, there's a serious problem with that wish, and it's the main reason I earned mostly "C's" in high school. Let me explain.

If you're a student in a college class, and you're just "hoping" you will pass the class, in all likelihood, what grade are you aiming for? Unanimously, in unison, students answer a "C." Because in all reality what is a "C"? It's a "passing" grade. If you get a "C" you're just happy you're still alive. However, the problem with this way of thinking can be hazardous to your GPA.

If you're aiming for a "C," like a goal, you have a 50/50 chance of achieving it. See how all this stuff ties in together. So there's a chance you will reach it, and there's a chance you won't. Now if you do reach this goal of a "C," you're happy, and you go on to the next class. But what happens if you miss your goal? More than likely, you will either hit a "D" or an "F." Has that ever happened to a student before? Probably more than we would like to admit. I know it happened to me a lot.

When I got to college, I knew I had to get off the "C-your-way-through-school" treadmill. So I asked myself, what would happen if I actually strived for an "A" in every class regardless of the level of difficulty? The answer almost made me drop dead after my first semester in college. I actually convinced myself not only that I would get an "A" in every class, but that I also "deserved" to get an "A" in every course regardless of the course. By the way, with a little change in my philosophy, I ended up pulling a 4.0 (17 credits) my first semester in college.

Sounds like a lot of positive thinking, right? Well that's part true. It also had to do with an unbelievable amount of faith in God and belief in myself.

I mentioned earlier in my introduction that teachers are human beings, and thus play favorites. That is true, but I don't believe God does. Why would God equip you with something and not equip me with similar tools. Given, your tools may be a little nicer and even sharper than mine, but we do have the same tools: a mind to think with, a heart to love with, and a soul to pray with. I just may need to spend more time polishing and sharpening my tools.

With that mentality, I asked myself in every class, has anyone ever made an "A" in this course before? If so, why couldn't I be the next? God assured me that I could. It was the most enlightening revelation of my academic life. I realized that college does not measure your intelligence, it measures your endurance. Remember? It's not about "IQ," but "I Will."

The highest possible grade in a class is an "A." That means that even the "not so bright ones" like me could get one. I say that facetiously, but I think you get the picture.

Let's look at the power behind raising your expectations. If you walk into that same tough course and "expect" to get an "A," there's a 50/50 chance you will get it, right? If you reach that goal, you will have astonished your friends, your parents, and maybe even yourself. Give yourself a pat on the back, and get ready for the next course. Now if you shoot for that "A," but you miss, what grade would you more than likely get from that class? You're right, you would probably earn a "B" or, at the worst, a "C." Does this make sense? See, it doesn't take a rocket scientist to figure this concept out. We don't get what we want, we get what we expect. You can never raise your standards by lowering your expectations.

Just to test this concept further, when I first started teaching at the college level, I asked all of my students on the first day of class two questions: 1.) How many of you "want" an "A" out of my course? and 2.) How many of you "expect" to get an "A" out of my course? When I asked the class the first question, usually 30 students out of 30 would raise their hand; but when I asked the class the second question, only 2 or 3 would raise their hand. Take a wild guess on how many received "A's" at the end of the semester? That's right, only 2 to 3. If that doesn't make my point clear, nothing will.

Well you might be saying, "Yeah Joe, I'm convinced, I need to raise my expectations in the classroom." But there's even more to this concept. As simple as the idea of raising your expectations may sound, I have something that's a little more radical to share with you. Let's re-examine the grading chart that I mentioned earlier.

A = **Excellent**
B = **Good**
C = **Average**
D = **Bad**
F = **Worst**

The New Grade Order

If you want to transform your grades, you can't stop at just raising your expectations, **you must also get rid of your college's ancient grading system.** I'm not saying you must do it physically by protesting, but rather mentally in the classroom. I believe it's a major reason why most students just barely graduate. It sets them up for failure by giving them too many options, especially if the school is on the plus and minus system. Let me explain.

When I internalized this concept of raising my expectations, I also set up my own grading system. The university could calculate my grades any way they wished, but I was going to hold myself accountable to a higher standard. I looked at their grading system and devised my own. Here it is:

A = Excellent
B = Good
F = Worst

This grading system, which only existed in my head, implied that if I received anything less than a "B" in any course, it was like failing. This may sound a little extreme, but guess what? It worked! I never earned anything less than a "B" in any course. I don't call that a coincidence; when you look at my scale, I never made a "C" or a "D" in a course because those grades didn't exist to me!

Believe it or not, most students use some mental form of this now, but their chart looks a little like this:

B = Lucky
C = Passing
D = Repeat
F = Fail

Students always asked me, why I used my A-B-F chart, and I usually give them two reasons:

1.) Quiet Desperation
Have you ever noticed how hard you worked in a class when you realized that you might miss a "C" and get a "D" in it? You were

willing to do whatever took to avoid repeating that course. You would study like someone promised you a million dollar reward or something. I know, I've been there. I just thought it would make sense to do it with my new grading system. Anytime I ever got close to not getting a "B," I would kick it into another gear. It was just a psychological thing. I can't explain it any better than that, but it worked.

2.) Common Sense
I was always happy making "C's" in high school until I discovered the true definition of a "C." Most would define a "C" as being average. And they would be right, but what is the true definition of the word "average"? Allow me to define it for you. If a person is average, that means they are better than the worst (i.e., D's and F's), right? But that would also mean that they are worst than the best (i.e., A's and B's), right? So if a "C" student is worst than the best and only better than the worst, doesn't that make them "Cream of the Crap"? Now, I don't know about you, but I'd rather not accept that as a compliment.

Those two reasons gave me the motivation I needed to design my own grading system. For the record, I don't want to imply that getting a "C" makes you any less than a human being. If the best grade you can earn in any class is a "C" (even a D or F for that matter), be proud of your effort. However, if you get a "C" or lower in a course (and you shouldn't if you apply these strategies), and you know in your heart you "could have" done better, you should be ashamed of yourself. I sure was embarrassed at my high school graduation. Don't be proud of your grades, be proud of your effort. Raise your standards by raising your expectations.

Quick Trick Action Steps: Break the Curve

1. Do whatever it takes to convince yourself that you can, will, and do deserve an "A" in every course.

2. Find out from the professor or another student if anybody ever earned an "A" in that particular class before (if not, go to Trick #5). If so, so can you.
3. Raise your expectations by adopting your own grading system (not your college's).
4. Make "C's" a thing of the past for you.
5. Put forth an effort you can be proud of, and graciously accept whatever grade you get.
6. Ask yourself: do I really <u>expect</u> to get an "A" in this course? If not, start from the top again.

Part II: Teacher Taming Techniques

In part one we started internally with your attitude, emotions, and beliefs about yourself and what you can accomplish in college. Without the three base builders, you have nothing to stand on. Now you do. Only <u>you</u> know if you've successfully adopted a strong why, concrete goals, and higher expectations.

Assuming you did internalize the three previous concepts, we can now kick this academic thing into overdrive. In the next few chapters, I will show you how you can get professors to become your personal coach and most loyal fans. I call this section "Teacher Taming Techniques." I know we're called professors, but I couldn't come up with an alliteration for the letter "P." Just work with me on this.

This section will show you how to position yourself for success and literally predict your grade in any course. Before we discuss them, understand that some techniques may be a little controversial and appear somewhat manipulative; but they are all legal and fall within the rules and guidelines of academia. However, I will warn you, these tricks will not work for the faint at heart; you must be willing to step out of your comfort zone.

Whereas the first part of this book takes commitment, the remainder of this book requires courage and common sense.

So if you're ready, let's begin.

Chapter 4: Let Your Fingers Do the Walking

Objectives:
1. Set yourself up for success by getting the best teachers.
2. Learn from other people's experiences, not your own.
3. Know your teachers before they know you.
4. Prepare for the obstacles before you encounter them.

Sometimes it's better to be lucky than good. During my second semester of my junior year in college, I had the misfortune of signing up for an economics course that was taught by a racist professor. How did I know he was racist? Well, after I had taken one of his tests, in which one of the questions was "What came first, the chicken or the egg (no joke)?" and I received a low score on it, I went by his office to see him. When I asked him about what I needed to do to earn an "A" in his class, he bitterly responded, "You people don't make A's in my course." Assuming I misunderstood him, I asked, "You mean our class?" He sharply responded, "No, I mean your people...blacks."

Needless to say I was floored; but I managed to adhere to the rule I gave you in the beginning of the book: never ever argue a grade. I just sucked it up and proceeded to work around him and his bigotry. It was tough, but my "WHY" was bigger than he was. After laboring through 16 weeks of his boring class, I ended up getting a B+, although I felt I deserved an "A." By the way, when he handed back our tests, it really wasn't the actual test, it was just a score with our name on it. That's right, I don't know if I ever got the chicken or the egg question right.

What does this have to do with Trick #4 and being lucky? Well, I couldn't believe what happened to me with this professor.

I was totally caught off guard to speak. I vowed never to let something like this happen to me again and not be prepared. I just didn't know what to do about it. This is where the luck came in.

One day I was searching for a friend's number I had lost. I turned my small apartment upside down, and I still couldn't find it. Fate would have it that I ran across a campus student directory. Almost every university has one. When I picked it up, I started to thumb through it for my friend's name. Within a matter of seconds I found his name listed. The information it had under his name just blew my mind. I'll change his name and address to protect his privacy, but this is basically what I saw:

John Doe
Major: Psychology
Class: Graduate Student
Address: 123 College Blvd.
          Jacksonville, FL 12345
Local Phone: 904-123-4567
Permanent: 904-123-4567

Now I don't know about you, but don't you think that's a little excessive? At least I thought so.

After I called him, I decided to look up my own name. What do you know, it had the same amount of information about me. It listed my major, classification, address, and both my local and hometown phone numbers. Just imagine it for a second. What if I looked your name up in the city directory, and it gave me your place of employment, how long you've worked there, and your work and home telephone numbers; would you be somewhat concerned? I know I would.

Well using my "common sense," I took a highlighter and went through that entire campus directory from A to Z, highlighting **every** student who was majoring in communications (like myself) who was at least a senior. Why seniors only? Because seniors are getting ready to graduate, and they've been through everything and anything along their four-year journey through college. They probably know about every professor, their hangups, their hot buttons, pet peeves, likes and dislikes, and whatever else you can think of. My question was why re-invent the wheel? I could learn from their mistakes and save myself a lot of time and a lot of frustration.

Think about the racist professor I mentioned earlier. Do you think I could have prepared myself better for him if I knew about him beforehand? You bet I could. Or even better, I could have avoided taking him in the first place; there were other economics professors available. I just didn't do my homework.

Well after I highlighted all of the seniors in my major, I drummed up some "courage," and let my fingers do the walking through the campus directory. I called each and every one of those students, approximately 50-something in all.

Using the script provided on the following pages, I was able to conduct a small research study on every professor in my department and even a few adjuncts. I even learned stuff I didn't even want to know about professors, like who was sleeping with who, what clubs certain professors usually frequented, who's in therapy and other outrageous information.

Usually when I share this strategy, students normally tell me, "I do something similar to that now; I ask my friends about professors." Understand me, this is not the same thing. I told you earlier that I contacted more than 50 students who were all seniors in my major. Asking a few of your closest friends about a professor is good, but it's not always reliable. First of all, your friend may not be in the same major. Your friend may think a professor is the greatest because she's interested in that particular subject; maybe your friend has a slightly higher aptitude; or maybe there was just some chemistry between the friend and the professor.

It also works in reverse if your friend disliked the professor. Your friend could have just been lazy that semester and is satisfied in blaming others. I think you get the picture.

With my method, if you talk to 25 seniors and five say

Professor Martin is great, and 20 say Professor Martin is the worst professor they've ever had, who are you more inclined to believe? In other words, the numbers don't lie. My research study not only proved to be reliable, it was darn near flawless. The information I got from those seniors was right on the mark. I never had another problem with a professor again, even the bad ones. I have a saying that goes, "It's easy to get yourself out of something if you know what you're getting yourself into."

Some colleges and universities now require that student evaluations (you know those things you fill out right before finals) be made public for all students. That's fine, but if you ever completed a student evaluation, you know the information only covers course content and teacher's ability. This type of information is okay (and I suggest you use it), but it doesn't give you a comprehensive picture of the entire situation.

On the contrary, my method not only gets you information about things on the surface (i.e., course content and teacher ability), but it also gets you information below the surface that student evaluations don't (i.e., professor pet peeves, tendencies, nuances, etc.). And most of all, it's reliable. These students are in your major, and they're all seniors. What a deal!

Below is an outline of Trick #4. You can deviate somewhat from the phone script, but follow the concept to the letter. Also note: this is definitely a strategy you want to keep to yourself. If everyone knew this trick, then it wouldn't work. Also, the seniors would probably get tired of all of those underclassmen calling their apartment. Be discreet.

Quick Trick Action Steps: Let Your Fingers Do the Walking

Steps Summarized:
1. Get a student/campus directory.
2. Get a highlighter (a different color per major).
3. Get a notepad and make a "T" in the middle of the page. Label "Bad"on the left, and "Good" on the right. (have a

blank page for additional notes)

4. Highlight ALL students who have the following characteristics:
     - Senior
     - In your major (or any other major in which you're having problems)
     - Have a local number listed (to avoid high telephone bills)
5. Rehearse script (practice, practice, practice)
6. Call each student highlighted using a script similar to the one below.

Example: **You:** Hello John, how are you?

Them: Let them respond.

You: John, my name is _____, and I'm a student at (name of college), and I'm new to the area. A student gave me your name and telephone number, and I'm so embarrassed, because for the life of me, I can't remember his name (I never wanted them to know I selectively picked their name out of a phone book -- you can tell them if you want to). Anyway, he suggested I give you a call. I didn't catch you at a bad time did I?

Them: If yes (request to call at a later time), If no, (continue).

You: John, if you don't mind me asking, what's your major?

Them: Let them respond.

You: Boy that's wild, so am I? (Pause) Are you a junior (or other classification) too?

Them: Let them respond.

You: (Enthusiastically) So you mean this is your last year/semester? I bet you're excited,

	aren't you?
Them:	Let them respond.
You:	I don't know if I'll ever graduate with the string of bad luck that I've had with professors so far. What did you think of the professors here at (name of your college)?
Them:	Let them respond.
You:	Any you regret taking? (If yes) -- Like who?
Them:	Let them respond. (Write down their responses on notepad -- BAD)
You:	What was so bad about them?
Them:	Let them respond. (Write down notes on separate sheet.)
You:	Who were your favorites?
Them:	Let them respond. (Write down their responses notepad -- GOOD)
You:	What was so good about them?
Them:	Let them respond. (Write down notes on separate sheet.)
You:	John, my roommate is giving me signals that he wants to use the phone. I've really enjoyed talking you. Thanks for being so helpful. Maybe, I'll get a chance to meet you before you graduate. Congratulations, and good luck.

Notes:

The keys to using this strategy are enthusiasm, sincerity, and friendliness. Don't be pushy. If they start spilling their guts about every professor and everything they know about them, don't say anything. . . let them speak. You just keep writing.

By the way, don't let them know that you're writing down all of this information. It would help even if you had a list of all of the teachers in your department (or a particular department) written down on a separate sheet of paper prior to the call. This way you could write a code (i.e., X for bad, Y for good, etc.) next to the appropriate name. If you don't have a list, just write very fast.

Chapter 5: The Secret Recipe

Objectives:
1. Make your first impression a lasting one.
2. Get "inside" information your classmates don't have..
3. Outline your strategy for achieving an "A."
4. Break professors' stereotypes of the "average student."
5. Make professors your biggest fan.

I am proud to say that this particular strategy is one of my favorites and also one of the most effective ones I've ever used. It's so simple that its remarkable that most students haven't tried it. Understand that all of the strategies listed in this book have proven to be effective at one time or another, but given the situation, some will work better than others. This one seemed to work almost all of the time.

The "Secret Recipe" was one of the first "tricks" I ever tried. It's kind of a misnomer to call it a trick, because it was never planned to be one. I attempted this strategy clearly out of sincere desperation and fear of screwing up in the classroom. It just so happens that after I used it, it worked a lot better than I ever anticipated. The "Secret Recipe" answered the age-old question for me, "Who would know best how to get an 'A' in any course?"

For this particular strategy, your confidence level will have to be at an all-time high. I'm not saying that mine was, but I faked it very well. It's like Les Brown once said, "sometimes you have to fake it until you make it." After I used this strategy the first time, it was much easier to use on subsequent occasions. You'll discover that this will apply to you as well.

Your First Day

One of the most anxious days in college, next to test day, is the infamous first day of class. On this particular day, students are nervous and professors are nervous (yes, teachers do get nervous -- remember, we're human too). Some students even make the critical mistake of not showing up on the first day or week of classes (see Trick #6).

On that first day, professors usually outline course requirements (i.e., give you a syllabus), give you their teaching philosophy, their background, answer student questions, and other boring stuff. Others even try to instill a little fear to weed out the slackers. Some professors deviate from the routine by giving tests or even allowing time for student introductions (a ploy to remember your name); but for the most part, there aren't many surprises.

On the first day of class, it is so important for you to make an initial positive impression on the professor. You obviously understand the consequences of a negative one; but most students don't understand that "no impression" is just as bad as a negative one. The reason this is true is because of our previous definition of average (i.e., cream of the crap). If a professor has no impression of you, he or she will assume you're probably just the "average student." The problem with this approach is the fact of what most professors (if not all) think of the "average student."

A better way to explain this point would be think about how you would describe the average college student yourself. Being totally honest, do you think the average college student is self-motivated, excited about his or her courses, eager to learn, striving to reach his or her full potential, loves to work hard, never makes excuses, is an eternal optimist, takes initiative, believes algebra is vitally important, etc? Guess what? Neither do we (professors).

With this in mind, you don't ever want to be classified as the "average" student. Therefore, you must do something positive to make a good, memorable impression on the professor. The larger the class, the more important this strategy is.

So how does this strategy work? The strategy is outlined in detail for you. Remember, look at what most students are doing or would do, and do the total opposite. You will succeed!

Quick Trick Action Steps: The Secret Recipe

Steps Summarized:
1. Stay after class on the first day.
2. Get a notepad.
3. Ask the professor for no more than ten (10) minutes of his or her time.
4. Ask the professor four (4) pre-prepared questions (see script).
5. Write down the professor's responses to questions 3 and 4 on your notepad.
6. Explain your purpose (why you're asking these questions) to your professor.
7. Thank professor for his or her time.

Example:

Setting -- It is the first day of class, and the professor has handed out the course syllabus, reviewed it, and has dismissed class. You intentionally stay after class as everyone leaves. Then casually approach the professor with your notepad in hand, using the following script:

You: Excuse me (professor's name), my name is John Doe, and I will be taking your class this semester. Do you have a few minutes?

Prof: No (reschedule a more convenient time).
Yes (proceed).

You: Thank you. I just wanted to ask

you a few questions before you go (wait for acknowledgment).

You: First of all, I'm really looking forward to taking this course. It appears we're going to be covering quite a bit of material.

You: If you don't mind me asking you, how long have you taught this particular course?

Prof: I guess it's been about seven years (of course, this will vary).

You: <u>Seven years</u>? That's great (pause). Well Dr./Professor _____, in the past <u>seven</u> years, has anyone ever earned an "A" in your course before?

Prof: Well, sure they have.

You: Great. What do you think they did to get an "A" in your course?

Prof: Well, I don't know -- maybe they _____, _____, _____, and _____. <Write down the professor's responses.>

You: Thanks. I have only one more question (wait for acknowledgment).

You: If <u>you</u> were a student in your class, what would <u>you</u> do to get an "A" in your class?

Prof: I really don't know, I've never really thought about it.

You: I know this may be an unusual question. But let me explain why I'm asking. I'm not the smartest student in your class. Matter of fact, I've never been the smartest student in any class. But, I know I can outwork anyone in any class. And I'm willing to work very hard for you. I just want to stay focused on the "right" things so I don't waste a lot of time majoring in minors. That's why I asked (pause).

You: (Give suggestions -- as many as you think of) Basically, what I'm asking is that if <u>you</u> were a student in <u>your</u> class, would you study the book more, concentrate more on the lectures, use your test bank to study, work in study groups, etc. What would be your strategy?

Prof: Well now that you mention it, I guess if I was student in my class, I would _____, _____, _____, and _____. <Write down the professor's responses.>

You: So let me get this right, you would _____, _____., _____, and _____.

You: Thank you very much for your time <shake hands>. I'll see you next class.

Notes:

The keys to using this strategy are sincerity, persistence, and attentiveness. Show the professor that your inquiries are sincere. Your only concern is doing your best, not to earn "brownie points" or to be a nuisance (make sure your body language and nonverbal communicate this).

Also, your professor will be caught off guard by your questions, and some of his/her responses will be vague. Get the professor to be as specific as possible. Don't settle for study hard, work hard, listen well. Study what? Work hard on what? Listen carefully to what?

Finally, as you get the professor to open up, listen very carefully to his/her responses. Listen between the lines, question things you're unclear about, and write down everything word for word. Repeat their responses to them if necessary.

Final Comments:

Most students who've tried this strategy are blown away by the results. Think about it? If you're getting information that all of your classmates don't have, you've already guaranteed yourself a letter grade better than most of the students in your class (given you apply the information the professor gave you).

The dangerous side of using this strategy is if you sought out this information insincerely. DON'T, and I repeat DON'T, ask your professor for this "secret recipe" if you have no intentions of using it. The worst thing you could do is get this information from your professor and not do what he or she told you to do. You would be committing nothing short of academic suicide. Harsh assessment you think? Well, ask yourself, if you were the professor, and a student tried this strategy on you only to prove later that he or she wasn't sincere about it, how would you feel? Not too good, would you? Remember, teachers are human beings too.

However, on the opposite side of that, if you diligently apply everything the professor told you, you will save a lot of time (no trial and error), you will have earned a fan (the professor), and you will receive a higher grade than you would have gotten otherwise (inside information).

The reason I like this strategy so much is not because it guaranteed me a letter grade better than the average, but because of the reputation I managed to build from it. Just ask yourself, what do you think professors thought of me after that first day of class? Do you think they thought I was unmotivated, not committed, irresponsible, not focused, not serious about my education, or just like the "average" student? No, they thought just the opposite.

Let the truth be told, the only thing I truly wanted to be called was "different." I just didn't want them to think I was like every other student in the class. Any other complimentary adjective they wanted to use to describe me was just icing on the cake. Be different!

Chapter 6: The School of Business

Objectives:
1. To get you to treat school like a job.
2. To position yourself for success.
3. To prosper from unmotivated students.
4. To build your credibility in the classroom.

As a professor, if there is one thing that concerns me more than anything else about students, it's the fact that most students treat school like a vacation (i.e., a social club) rather than a vocation (i.e., a job). This is not to say that you shouldn't have fun in college. That's like saying you shouldn't have fun at work. Not only is that ridiculous, it's stressful. On the contrary, I mean that you need to accept college for what it is, a business.

Think about it, as a customer, don't you pay money for your college's services? Don't you get something back for your money (at least that's what you hope)? Don't you have the option to spend your money (i.e., tuition) anywhere you choose? Can't you complain to administration if you feel that you've been mistreated? Are you starting to get my point?

Now let's look at it from the employee's (your) standpoint. In college, aren't you held accountable by someone in an authority position? Do these authority figures sometimes get on your nerves? If you do not perform up to par or do not demonstrate the basic competencies to perform, will you get promoted (i.e., pass the class)? Don't you sometimes feel like you're being overworked? I don't know about you, but this sounds like a job to me.

The point is this, if you want a sure way to ace college, treat school more like a job than a four-year stint at summer camp. I could tell you many stories about how my classmates never took this concept to heart. They just went aimlessly from one class to another, not worrying about how they were being perceived by their professors (i.e., reputation) or how their reputation determined what kind of grades they would receive at the end of the semester.

I will attempt to explain this "school is a business" concept, and I will share a personal story with you on how I benefitted from it. Just remember, all of these tricks and strategies tie in together.

Ask yourself this, "if you missed work every other week or you were late to work every other day, what would happen to you?" Right after you were warned, you would eventually get fired if it continued to happen. However, in college, professors can't fire you, but they can fail you. In a nutshell, treat school like a business (i.e., job) and show up; and show up on time.

Here's another example; if my boss gave me an assignment, and I constantly complained about it, consistently missed deadlines, made numerous excuses for not completing it, and it was less than professional when I finally submitted it, what would happen to me? I'll make it easier for you, what wouldn't happen to me? I wouldn't get any promotions, raises, or bonuses. My boss would lose all trust and confidence in me. Matter of fact, it would probably be best if I started looking for another job.

If you do any of these things that I mentioned earlier, guess what? You don't get that promotion (i.e., pass), you ruin your reputation, and you don't get that raise you wanted (i.e., an A or B). Is it starting to sink in?

When I say you need to treat school like a business, I mean **REALLY** treat it like a business. Respect your employer (your professor) whether or not you like him or her; turn in all assignments on time; turn in professional-looking work; accept responsibility for your mistakes and screw-ups; have an eagerness to learn; keep a positive attitude and anything else you could possibly think of. Sounds tough? Hey, no one ever said college would be easy.

The Golden Rule

When I was in college, I mastered this "School of Business"

technique by remembering what my mama always told me, "Joe, if you treat people the way you want to be treated, you'll never have to worry about having people problems." Mama and the Bible were right, "Do unto others as you have them do unto you." The one thing I'm most proud of as a student is the fact that **I NEVER** turned in an assignment late, and I never failed to complete one. Unfortunately, most of my classmates couldn't make that same claim. Imagine telling your boss, "Oh, that assignment you gave me, I forgot about it and didn't do it; or do I get extra credit for doing my job?"

Remember, in the end your credibility (reputation) will almost always earn you one letter grade higher than you deserve. Just think about it, have you ever received a grade higher than you thought you actually earned? Now ask yourself, what did that professor think of you? More than likely, it was positive. This book is not rocket science; almost anybody can apply these strategies. I'm appealing to your common sense here.

Personally, I know I received at least one grade higher than I actually earned in at least a third of my classes. You don't think that had an effect on my grade point average? I am certain that these "grade bonuses" were a result of my credibility as a hard working student in the classroom. Remember, just like a job, reputation counts.

The fact of the matter is, whether you treat school like a business or not, your professors will. We're trying to prepare professionals for the workforce, and the first step is to treat you like you're already a professional. I'm just suggesting that you make an effort to be worthy of being called a "professional."

Unlike the other previous (as well as the following) "tricks," this particular strategy should be common practice. No one, including professors, should have to ask students to act like professionals. As a college student, your integrity and character shouldn't allow you to act in any other way. I tell my students that your character is who you are when nobody's looking. I personally believe that we could double, maybe even triple, the national graduation rate if students treated college more like a business.

Yes, you pay your money, so you have the right to treat school any way you wish. But when was the last time you bought something from Walmart (i.e., college) and the employees (i.e., professors) got a chance to evaluate you (the customer) afterwards? Given this fact, when was the last time employees rated you poorly (i.e., a failing grade), didn't give you what you paid for (i.e., a passing grade), and then asked you to come back tomorrow and pay for it all over again? Sounds ridiculous doesn't it? But isn't that the way the college business is run? You pay your money, most of the time you don't get what you paid for, you get treated like crap, you're offered no guarantees, and even if you don't like it, you have to come back tomorrow, next week, or maybe next year and pay even more for it. What a business! I wish they sold stock.

Trust me on this one, it pays (i.e., better grades) to treat school like a business.

The Right Place at the Right Time

Allow me to share a personal story with you. I was enrolled in a Tuesday evening (5:00 p.m.) marketing course with one of the most boring professors I've ever seen in my life. The class lasted until 8:30 p.m. (thank God it was only one night a week). This professor would stand before the class and "read" the contents of the chapters (word for word) for over three hours in the most monotone voice I've ever heard. No joke! Since we only met once a week, very few students blew off his class, even though they probably could have (I believe everyone in our class was literate).

During this same semester, Janet Jackson had come to town to practice for a concert in a neighboring city approximately 60 miles away. When the local media found out about it, the public demanded that Janet give a concert in our city. After much haggling between her promoters and our city officials, Janet agreed to give a one-day concert at a discount rate of $10 per ticket. The city was excited!

However, the date and time of the concert was on a Tuesday at 5:30 p.m. We're talking about a concert during the middle of rush hour, right after work, and most importantly, in direct conflict with my class schedule.

Now understand, being a young man with testosterone bursting out of my ears, this was a dream come true. I thought Janet Jackson was hotter than the heat in Miami, and I'm not talking about the basketball team. Even the $10 ticket price was within my budget; so this became the event I just couldn't afford to miss.

Even after I realized that her concert schedule was in direct conflict with Professor "Snoring's" class, I had already decided to skip his class. But on the day before the concert, I took a glimpse at my notes in my school folder and I saw my **"WHY STATEMENT"** staring me right in the face. I asked myself, "Joe, are you here (in college) to watch Janet shake her butt on stage, or are you here to find a way to get your mother and sister out of the ghetto?" There's no need to tell you what the right answer was. So in total disgust, I decided to let my image of Janet Jackson bouncing around on stage bounce right out of my head.

Of course when Tuesday night came, I didn't have the greatest attitude in class. To make matters worse, our class of 35 shrunk to just three on that evening. I never saw anything like it. I guess almost everyone was a Janet Jackson fan (or at least for that night). Our class looked like a ghost town.

When the professor came in, it appeared he didn't even notice that we were the only three students there. In fact, it wasn't until fifteen minutes had passed when he sneezed and looked up and noticed that the classroom was basically empty. I told you, this guy was out of it. He asked, "Where's everybody?" And one kid in the back said, "I think they're all at the Janet Jackson concert tonight." I guess telling on his fellow classmates was his way of getting back at them for having fun. Professor "Snoring" (as I will lovingly call him) then responded surprisingly, "Oh, that's where they are?" And what he proceeded to do next just blew me away.

"Well, I want each of you to take out a sheet of paper, " he continued. "We're going to have a pop quiz."

Needless to say, I was ticked off. Not only did I miss my date with Janet Jackson (hey, a man can dream can't he?), this guy was giving us a quiz that I didn't even prepare for. Whoever said that life wasn't fair should be shot for making such an understatement.

Professor "Snoring" continued to tell us, "Before you take the quiz, I want you to write in the top right-hand corner, from 0 to 100%, what you think you deserve to get on this quiz. Then I want you to write your name under the score you wrote," he concluded.

Even though I didn't study for this test, I still I believed I deserved to get an "A" on it, so I wrote down 100%. Remember what I said earlier about "Breaking the Curve"? You can't raise your standards by lowering your expectations. Besides, what was wrong with a little wishful thinking?

He then proceeded to walk around the class, and he asked us to hand the paper to him. He said, "This quiz will count for 25% of your grade."

After I was able to breathe again, I realized what had just happened. I got a 100% percent for just showing up and putting my name on a sheet of paper. The thought of Janet Jackson on stage seemed so insignificant at that moment in time. The $10 I saved from not going to the concert, I eventually used to purchase her cassette (couldn't afford the CD).

What was funnier was what happened in our class the following week. When the students, now about 30 or so in attendance, found out that we had a pop quiz that was worth 25% of our grade (and no chance for a make up exam), they went ballistic. They wanted to start a revolt, claiming that the professor couldn't do what he did.

Given the fact that this professor had tenure (i.e., the ultimate in job security), those students had a better chance of getting the university to change its name than they did getting him to change their grade. Needless to say, he didn't budge an inch.

That semester, over half the class failed that course, and they all had to take him again (he was the only professor teaching that section). Yours truly pulled a B+ (hey, I'm not perfect), which was also the highest grade in the class. This is just an example of what can happen to you if you fail or succeed in treating school like a job. Please, don't learn the hard way.

Listed are some simple rules that any student can follow. The great speaker/philosopher, Jim Rohn, once said, "Those things that are easy to do are also easy not to do." This is unfortunate, but also very true. If you work to become the "employee of the semester" in every class you take, I guarantee you that both you and your grades will get promoted.

Quick Trick Action Rules: The School of Business

1. Try to show up for class every day even when you don't feel like it.

Before you decide not to go to class due to sickness or whatever reason, ask yourself, "Would I stay home today if I knew the professor was giving us a test today with no chance for a makeup?" If the answer is "yes," stay home. If the answer is "no," read your "WHY STATEMENT," get off your butt, and get going!

2. Be on time!

Remember what I said earlier, what would happen if you showed up to work late every other day or even once a week? That's right, you'd get fired. Don't get fired from school, get fired up about school.

3. Accept personal responsibility for everything that happens to you.

Even if it's not your fault, accept responsibility. You will earn the respect of your peers and your professors. Your peers may not be in a position to do anything for you, but your professors are. I could share numerous stories how this has paid off for me (as a student) and my students in the long run.

4. Type everything, and do it neatly and professionally.

Even if the professor doesn't specify, type it. And if you really want to get on their good side, put a cover page on it. Remember, do what most students aren't willing to do. Unfortunately, your academic success will depend on their (other students) laziness or lack of motivation. Hey, I didn't write the rules, that's just the way it is.

5. Proofread everything until you're tired of reading it, and then proofread it again.

The professional student rarely turns in a paper with typos. You can't always trust "spell check," so don't. Get others you can trust to double-check your work. Also, avoid making last minute corrections on your paper in ink. To avoid this, after you get to class, don't proofread your paper anymore. Do your proofreading before you get to class, not in class. This will also help you to reduce stress.

6. Never, never, never argue a grade (refer to number 3).

You might win the battle (i.e., a higher grade), but I can tell you as a professor, you WILL lose the war (i.e., no letter of recommendation, no benefit of the doubt grade boost at the end of the semester, no great internship leads, no connection with their network, no favorable comments about your character, etc.). Trust me, it's not worth it.

7. Turn ALL assignments in on time.

Since I never turned in an assignment late before, I have to plead my ignorance on what to do if you just "have to" turn one in late. My solution was, even if I wasn't there, my assignment was going to be there. Complete the assignment early if you have to; get others to drop it off for you (but make sure they're reliable; and double-check with your professor to make sure he or she received it). Just do whatever it takes as if your life depended on it. Guess what? Nobody else is willing to go through the trouble, so that means the professor will be highly impressed because he or she doesn't expect it from you.

I remember one time when I Federal Expressed my assignment to a professor when I was out of town (although I had to borrow the money to do it). You don't think she was impressed by that? By the way, I received an "A" in her class with an 86 overall average. You figure the math. I'm telling you, reputation counts!

8. Always do a little more than the average student will do.

If you follow all of the previous seven rules listed, you <u>will</u> be going the extra mile. The extra mile includes preparing cover pages for all assignments, turning in assignments a day early (I've given students higher grades just because of that), and utilizing the professor's office hours (it gets lonely in our office). Again, a full-proof method of going the extra mile is to ask yourself, "What would the typical student do in a situation like this?" Whatever answer you conclude, do the total opposite. It never fails.

Notes:

The key to using this strategy is professionalism. Always pretend you're an up and coming executive at a Fortune 500 company. Do things with style, class, and professionalism. Make yourself standout among your peers by going the "extra mile." No one has ever gotten lost going the extra mile. And you might as well get use to it now because that's what's expected of you in the "real world." School isn't any different. If you show your professor you deserve a raise (i.e., a higher grade), believe me, you will get it.

Bonus: "Student Stranglers"

Staying with the philosophy that you need to treat school like a business (i.e., a job), I decided to throw in a special section to help you see the picture a little clearer. Listed below, with a brief explanation of each, are 16 categories in which college professors place their students. In a sense, you could call it stereotyping or prejudging, but we all do it -- we're human for goodness sake. I'm not saying that it's right or that it's fair, but it happens. I call these categories the "Student Stranglers" because they strangle your chances for success in the classroom.

Not all of these categories are weighted equally (it depends on the temperament of the professor), but they all should be taken seriously. Please listen to me, you need to **AVOID THEM AT ALL COSTS!** Your professors will not tell you which category they've placed you in, so your job (your mission) is NOT to put yourself in any one of them. Browse the list to see if you or any of your friends are guilty of falling into one or more of these "Student Strangler" categories. If you do, get out of them!

Professor Prejudices	
ButtSharks	**Definition:** students who choose brown-nosing as both their major and their minor. **Famous Words:** (Any type of ingratiating compliments) **Solution:** Avoid complimenting professors, unless it's about the subject matter or their commitment to teaching.

Excuser Losers	**Definition:** students who blame everyone and everything, including the weather, for their bad grades. **Famous Words:** "Let me tell you or explain to you want happened..." **Solution:** Accept responsibility (even if it wasn't your fault).
The Whiners	**Definition:** students who complain about every assignment, project, group, grade, class, and/or incurable disease. **Famous Questions:** "Why do we have to...?" **Solution:** Stop complaining! Keep your complaints to yourself, unless asked.
Johnny-Come-Latelies	**Definition:** students who have watches that are set 10 minutes slower than everyone else's (they are always late to class). **Famous Words:** "I got caught up in traffic or I overslept or my alarm didn't go off." **Solution:** Strive to get to class five minutes early.
Echo Experts	**Definition:** students who comprehend only after the 99th time the answer or point has been repeated. **Famous Words:** "Can you repeat that? One more time please. I didn't get that last point." **Solution:** If it's necessary for the professor to repeat something for you more than twice, see him/her about it after class.

Mike Tysons	**Definition:** students who like to fight or bite your ear off about their grades. **Famous Words:** "He/She (the Professor) can't get away with that. That's not fair." **Solution:** Suck it up (concede the battle, but win the war) or question the professor tactfully in private. But don't ever argue.
Paranoid Floyds	**Definition:** students who think the professor and the U.S. government are strategically plotting to fail them. **Famous Words:** "I really think the professor is out to get me (or doesn't like me)." **Solution:** Get over it.
Einstein Rejects	**Definition:** students who act like THEY should be teaching the course, instead of the professor. **Famous Words:** "I have a lot of experience in that area. I know lot about that." **Solution:** Use your knowledge to impress people outside of the classroom, not in it.
Fed-Ex Rejects	**Definition:** students who absolutely, positively, couldn't turn in an assignment on time if their life depended on it. **Famous Words:** "Can I get an extension (extra time) on that deadline." **Solution:** Strive to turn in your assignment a day early.

Geraldo Riveras	**Definition:** students who have the need to get the last word in on every subject. **Famous Words:** "I have something to say about that. I disagree with that. I have an opinion on that." **Solution:** If the professor doesn't ask for your opinion, don't give it.
Jim Carey Wannabees	**Definition:** students who will do or say anything for a laugh. **Solution:** Only strive to get a laugh if someone is going to pay you for it.
The Peekaboos	**Definition:** students who show up for class only on test day or when there's free food. They've never seen the inside of a professor's office before. **Solution:** Get your money back for the course.
The Whispers	**Definition:** students who professors have to threaten or blackmail to get them to speak up and participate in class. **Famous Responses:** "I don't know. I have nothing to say about that." Complete silence. **Solution:** Prove that you're breathing, speak up.
Creditor Predators	**Definition:** students who want extra credit for everything, including blowing their nose, spelling their name correctly, and staying awake in class. **Famous words:** "Do we get extra credit for that?" **Solution:** Never ask for extra credit. If you do what you have to, you'll never need it.

Stalkers	**Definition:** those who stick to professors like bad habits. Wherever you see the teacher, you see the student. **Solution:** Give professors their space. There are laws against stalking. Use the professor's office hours for personal visits.
The Clueless	**Definition:** students who have no idea what's going on in class. The only thing they're concerned about is spring break and school holidays. They usually ask other students a million questions about what's going on. **Famous Questions:** "So, what are we doing now? What was the assignment again? Did you get the class notes?" **Solution:** Follow the advice given to the Peekaboos, get your money back.

Note: *I'm absolutely certain that there are more categories than the ones listed above. What do you think? However, I'm equally certain that any additional categories are equally as negative.*

Students always ask me, "All of these categories are negative, where are the positive categories?" My response to them is: **THERE AREN'T ANY.** The reason there aren't any positive categories for students is because there aren't enough positive students to place in them. I know that sounds harsh, but it's the truth.

Just think about the categories you just reviewed, didn't you think of at least one or more students who could be categorized in each of the categories?

Your mission, as I mentioned earlier, is to **AVOID THESE AT ALL COSTS.** However, that's not all you need to do. Not only do you need to avoid all of these categories, you need to also **CREATE** a positive new category for yourself, and that category is called **DIFFERENT**. Even if your teacher doesn't know who you are, it's just as bad as being placed in a negative category. Don't forget what I told you about what professors think of most college students.

What I'm saying is that it's better to be categorized as **DIFFERENT** than not to be categorized at all. The "tricks" you learned earlier are about setting yourself apart (being "different") from the rest of your classmates.

Everything that you've done up until this point with the "Tricks of the Grade" is different than what most of your friends and other students are doing. Would you agree? And what did I say earlier, if you want to be a successful college student, just observe what most students are doing, and do the total opposite (however, keep it legal). The fact is, if you do what most students do, you will get what most students get, average grades.

Chapter 7: Boring is Better

Objective:

1. Take advantage of a human glitch in the education system.
2. Get better grades in tougher courses.
3. Get better grades in boring courses.
4. Pad your GPA during the school's down time.

Well, you've made it this far, and some of the tricks have been intense. If you've applied some of these strategies before finishing the book, you're probably starting to understand why these strategies work so effectively. You've figured out that the key to college success is doing the opposite of what most students would do (given the same situation).

However, this next strategy is not as intense as the others. Matter of fact, it doesn't require you to "do things differently," but rather to "think differently." I call this "Boring is Better."

This has to be the easiest "trick" you can apply while you're in college. Again, most students don't know about it. Like the others, I kind of stumbled across this one by accident too. Easy isn't the only thing that separates this strategy from the others, it's the fact that I couldn't prove this one until "after" I became a professor.

"Boring is Better" supports my theory that classes offered over the summer term are usually easier. *Therefore, I believe you should always take your toughest and most boring courses over the summer terms.*

Although I can't see you, I can feel you squirming in you chair with a perplexed look on your face. Your argument might be, "Summer terms are usually shorter, so wouldn't that make the class <u>more</u> difficult?" You might even add, "Who in their right mind would want to take physics or calculus crammed into 6 or 12 weeks?"

These, and any other arguments you might have, would all be

legitimate, but allow me to prove why boring is always better. There are two key points to make.

Boring is Better Rationale

First, if you were here standing next to me, and I started punching you in your arm with all my strength, but you couldn't go anywhere, would you rather I punch you in the arm for six weeks or 16 weeks? Now, you're probably saying, "I wouldn't want you to punch me at all," but the reality is that as long as you're a college student, you will get punched. The only option you have is for how long? Therefore, I would suggest you choose to get "punched" by that boring or tough professor or course for a shorter duration. It only makes common sense (I told you it would come in handy).

Second (and this is something I found out after I became a professor), a college professor is usually on a nine-month contract. That means that most professors get summers off. I found out that most professors usually decide to teach during the summer for one or two reasons. The first reason is to earn extra money. Hopefully, that doesn't come as a surprise to you; but the second reason might. If professors don't need to earn extra money, they may choose to teach over the summer to finish projects they started during the fall and spring terms (i.e., writing a book, doing research, etc.) Having access to their office computer and campus resources can really be a big plus for them; not to mention, being in an academic environment helps them stay focused.

The second point is so critical because if professors are primarily focused on earning extra money or completing their books and research projects, who are they NOT focusing on? That's right, YOU! Unfortunately, students are third on the priority list. I mentioned early in the book that teachers are human beings. If you believe that, ask yourself this question, "If you were a professor, and you needed to earn extra money and/or complete your research project, would you bust your hump teaching if your two primary goals were already guaranteed?" I didn't think so.

It is human nature not to work hard if you don't really have to and especially if there's no incentive. Don't just take my word for it, ask any of your friends.

The ironic thing is this, since the summer semesters are shorter, it actually requires more work on the professor's part to prepare. However, very few professors put forth that effort. The exception to my theory is adjunct professors (those who teach part-time). They have nothing to lose, they already have an outside job that pays them more than teaching does; they don't have to publish any books or articles to keep their jobs, so they're only focus is you. Avoid adjuncts at all costs during the summer.

On the other hand, those nine-month professors, who find themselves having to squeeze their 16-week course into 12 or six weeks, understand that unless they shave some of the requirements (the key concept here), creating a thorough course would be like mission impossible.

Hindsight is 4.0/4.0

As a student, I figured this strategy out by accident (like most of them). I happened to review a copy of my college transcript during my junior year. I noticed that I never made anything less than an "A" during the summer term (which I always attended). However, I had taken my toughest and most boring courses over the summer. It just didn't make any sense, until I figured it out.

During the fall and the spring term, when students may have to take four tests in any given class, that same class may require only two tests if taken over the summer. The professor who requires you to write five papers during the course of the fall and spring terms, may only require you to do two or three during the summer term.

Are you following the logic here? No professor worth their salt can look themselves in the mirror with a clear conscience and expect you to thoroughly understand in six weeks what their previous classes "couldn't" learn in 16 weeks. The only logical solution would be to reduce the requirements, relax a little on the details, inflate the grades to balance the scales, or whatever strategy he or she can come up with to have a clear conscience.

If you don't believe this happens, explain to me how a student in high school can fail 36 weeks of math and English and go to summer school and pass both classes in only six to eight weeks? No one ever said the system was perfect. I'm just telling you to allow the system to work for you instead of against you. It's already set up in your favor.

Quick Trick Action Rules: Boring is Better

Steps Summarized:
1. Take all of your boring and tough classes over the summer.
2. Don't take more than two courses per summer session (term).
3. Sign up for summer classes taught by full-time professors only (avoid adjuncts).
4. Use Trick #4 (The Recipe) on this professor.

Notes:

The key to using this strategy is common sense. This is the easiest trick to use and one of the best kept secrets to raise your GPA. Unfortunately, most students don't know about it. This is a strategy that will make you look back and ask yourself, "How come I didn't think of this before?"

The only thing that can stand in your way now is your need for a school break (which you probably deserve). I always enrolled in summer courses, and I ended up graduating college in 3 ½ years! But you have to ask yourself, "What's more important to me, a vacation or my graduation?" By the way, there's no wrong answer. Just understand that you do have a choice.

Chapter 8: The Good Book

Objectives:
1. To make your first impression a lasting one.
2. To tame the "Nightmare Professor."
3. To give you an unfair advantage over your peers.

Tired of that one professor you can't avoid? You know the one -- he teaches the toughest course in your major or is the toughest professor in your major, and he is the only one that teaches it. What do you do? Should you pray and hope that the professor gets ill during the term you have to enroll for his course? Should you stick around for 10 years until he retires? Should you just pay the professor a bribe before the term begins? (Hmm, now that might work -- just kidding.) Don't worry, I have a solution for you, and it won't cost you any money; it's called "The Good Book."

This is another one of those strategies that colleges will never teach you in student orientation. It works phenomenally.

I must tell you that this next strategy has gotten me in a lot of trouble with my friends. It's a strategy you definitely cannot share with your friends (no matter how close you are). If you and every other soul tried this strategy on the same professor (especially during the same term), it wouldn't work. But nobody has to know this trick except for you and me, right?

When one thinks of the phrase "The Good Book," they think of the Bible. Well, the Bible in this case is your syllabus. What does the syllabus have to do with your "Professor Nightmare on Elm Street?" Everything! The syllabus is your success meal ticket out of this professor's class. How, you ask?

Go back to my premise that your grades are not important, but your reputation is. This professor that you can't avoid has a reputation that precedes her. The class is almost impossible to pass; the workload is too heavy; the professor is difficult to understand; her expectations are too high; and the list goes on and on. It shouldn't surprise you that if you've heard a lot about this professor and how disliked she is, the professor has heard the same things too.

I hate to say this, but he or she probably doesn't care too much about you either. Professors have feelings too you know. If they feel someone doesn't like them, guess what, they will withdraw into their shell like a turtle. That's where the syllabus comes in -- it brings them out. Let me explain.

The Power of the Book

The course syllabus is your invitation to make an impression on the professor who nobody likes. What amazes me more than anything is how few students ever take the time to read the course syllabus. Professors literally slave over outlining the requirements of their course, making sure there are no misunderstandings, to only find out later that the first day of class will probably be the last time most students will ever look at the syllabus. This is wrong. **Read, study, and know your syllabus.** Ask your professors questions about it. It will literally shock them. Trust me on this.

Let me tell you something that very few students know; nothing ticks off a professor more than when a student asks a specific question about the course that's already covered in the syllabus. Take it from me, it's like screaming "That's right, I'm lazy!" in the professor's ear. Remember, guard your reputation.

This strategy requires you to request a copy of the professor's syllabus a semester before you take him or her. It doesn't matter if the syllabus will change, whether or not the professor is out of them, or whatever. All that matters is that you request one (the semester before). Why request one before you take the class, to make an impression on the professor.

Do you remember all of those things you heard about that professor from other students? Well let me share with you what that same professor is probably thinking about you (not you personally, but students collectively):

"These students are lazy, unmotivated, and they don't appreciate good professors like me. Anybody could pass my course if they took their education seriously. I don't see how these students got admitted to college in the first place. I know one thing, I don't care how many times they have to take this course, they're going to learn this material, even if it kills me (or them)."

Exaggerated? maybe a tad, but it's not that far from the truth. The point here is that you are not seen in a positive light, and the professor hasn't even met you yet! Those are not good odds. My advice is to get the odds in your favor "before" you start running the race. The way you do that is to make a positive, memorable impression with something as small as requesting a course syllabus (the semester before).

So, how can you be sure this strategy will do it? Because no one, and I mean no one, will attempt this unless you tell them about it. I know, I did it, and it works; I have the bitter friends to prove it.

Meet Dr. Robo-B!*#%

Let me share a personal example of this strategy in action. At my university, in my department, we had a professor who had a reputation that even "Jack the Ripper" would have been proud. She stood about 5 feet 1 inch tall, 115 pounds, with short dark black hair, and she was pale as a ghost. She never wore even a smudge of make-up. She was as emotionless as someone missing the winning lotto number by one digit. She never smiled, she never engaged students in conversations in or outside of the classroom, and this was on a "good" day.

The rumor was that most students had to take her class an average of 2.78 times to pass it. To make matters worst, she was the only professor teaching the three sections that were offered each semester.

This particular professor had earned the dubious name, Dr. Robo-B#%! I'll let you fill in the blanks (it rhymes with witch). Students shuddered at the very sound of her name. She was tough, she was relentless, and she was very serious about her job.

Knowing this, I knew eventually the time would come when I had to take her class. But being a student of the "Tricks of the Grade," I was not a bit concerned. As a matter of fact, I was even a little cocky about taking her. I told some of my friends (in the spring term) that I would take her class during the summer (Trick #7).

To my friends' amazement, they couldn't understand why, and I wouldn't tell them either. I never shared my tricks with my classmates (it's your choice if you do). I also told them that I would pull an "A" out of her class. This, you could imagine, floored them.

Little did my friends know, I had a plan. Even my roommate, who was taking the same class for the second time, didn't know about my plan. I had one of my other previous professors request a copy of Dr. Robo's course syllabus for me the semester before the course. Why did I do that you ask? Like I said before, I wanted to make a positive impression on her.

I had already heard from other students how tough she was. She had an extensive reading list that she assigned at the beginning of the semester (extensive was an understatement -- there were at least 10 to 15 books of required reading). Remember, this was a six-week summer course! I also heard that all of her tests were composed of detailed essay questions. To make matters worse, I heard that she would call on students randomly every five minutes asking questions about the reading assignments from the list. No wonder everyone was scared of her. So I pulled out all the stops (tricks) on her, including this particular one.

The other professor I mentioned earlier agreed to get a copy of Dr. Robo's syllabus for me. When I went to pick it up, I asked the professor, what did Dr. Robo think of my request? The professor replied, "She asked me, 'what kind of student would

request a copy of a course syllabus a semester before the class?'"
Even though it wasn't scripted, my kind professor responded, "I
don't know, but Joe Martin is a different kind of student."
Bingo! -- exactly the type of response I was looking for. I
thanked the professor for getting the information for me, and I
left her office with a huge grin on my face.

See, although I never met Dr. Robo personally, I knew now
that I would never have a problem approaching her about
anything. Why not? Because the ice had been broken. I knew
she would never forget Joe Martin. Now, with syllabus in hand,
all I had to do was wait for the semester to begin.

The Day of Reckoning

On the first day of class, to my amazement, the room was
filled to capacity. I guess the word had gotten out that I was
bragging how I was going to ace Dr. Robo's class the first time
around. Maybe they thought I knew something they didn't. They
were right, I did.

The room was deafening with noise as students bragged
about their two and three-term stints with Dr. Robo as if it were a
prison sentence. Some were discussing strategies on what it
would take to pass her course, and others (the clueless) couldn't
even remember what she taught. By the way, she taught
communication ethics and law.

As Dr. Robo entered the classroom, a scary silence fell over
the room. No one said a word, including me. It's like you could
hear her footsteps as she made her way to the podium. As she
opened her lecture folder, which was as thick as a Webster
Dictionary (the unabridged edition), we watched her like sheep
ready for the slaughter.

She started calling class roll. Like a machine gun, she read
aloud each student's name. Each student responded with an
emotionless...here!...here!...here! Then something strange
happened. Dr. Robo called my name, and after I responded like
my peers...here!...she abruptly stopped. "Where is Joe Martin?"

she asked. "I'm right here," I said. And in unison, every student in the classroom, including my roommate, all turned their heads and stared at me in amazement.

The professor asked, "Did Professor 'Such and Such' give you that information you requested?" I replied, "Yes she did, thank you." The class was dumbfounded and speechless. My roommate leaned over to ask me about the information, "What information is she talking about?" I told him I'd tell him about it later (I never did).

He then asked me if I knew her. "Joe, she smiled at you man," he said. "I've never seen her smile at a student before, and this is my third time taking her." I ensured him that I didn't know her and that I had never met her before in my life. He didn't buy it.

After class, after all of the students had left, I went up to Dr. Robo and employed Trick #5: The Recipe. It worked brilliantly. I won't even go into the details of why most students usually failed her course, but she told me. Needless to say, we built a good student-teacher relationship. She gave me the information I needed to get an "A" in her course, I applied them, and I got an "A" in the course on my "first time" around.

It was obvious, as my roommate kept reminding me, that she treated me differently than everyone else. To my peers, it just didn't make sense.

Dr. Robo in Hindsight

I think it should be repeated here again, your grades are not important, but your reputation is. Let me let you in on another secret. I never even looked at that syllabus after the other professor had gone through all the trouble of getting it for me; I planned to, but I didn't have time. That was the only mistake I made with this strategy (don't you do the same).

In the summary, I've worked out the kinks to make this strategy even more effective for you.

The point is this, Dr. Robo treated me differently because I

WAS different. I stepped out of my comfort zone to do what most students weren't willing to do, which was think of her as a human being, not a machine. To her, I was indeed different.

I never told my friends what I did to get an "A" in her class until I graduated. And I must confess, some are still a little mad at me. But any one of them could have done exactly what I did in that class, and now you can too. All it takes is sizing up the competition and asking yourself, what would most students do, and then do the opposite. I guarantee you, more times than not, you will win, and win big!

Quick Action Steps: The Good Book

Steps Summarized:
1. Set up an appointment to meet the professor in his or her office.
2. Ask to see the professor's syllabus the semester before you enroll.
3. Explain your purpose to the professor (i.e. to be prepared, get a quick start, etc.).
4. Ask about and request any assigned reading material.
5. Ask him or her how should you effectively prepare for the class (and then do it).
6. Quickly scan the syllabus and ask questions if you have any.
7. Thank the professor for his or her time.

Notes:

The key to using this strategy is preparation. Know your objective before approaching the professor. Be sincere, persistent, and pleasant. Don't brown nose, and don't give compliments. Be professional and be serious. Also, don't forget to ask questions about the syllabus while you're in their office.

Your professor may be caught off guard, but he or she WILL be impressed. That's your aim. Make the teacher curious, and you WILL succeed.

Part III: Street-Smart Study Strategies

In part two, I had you step out of your comfort zone to really set yourself apart from other students. It's usually during the step two process that most students quit on me. As I mentioned in the introduction, these tricks take courage. That's why Trick #1 was so important. If you don't have a strong enough "WHY," any excuse will do for not attempting these strategies. I have to admit, if I wasn't so desperate and scared of college, I wouldn't have been brave enough to try them myself.

However, I didn't have a choice, and neither did my family. Courage is something I cannot teach you. The good news is that the two remaining strategies do not require as much courage. However, they do require a strong dose of commitment. They are absolutely awesome, and like the others, they are pretty easy to implement.

Again, I must warn you, some students may describe these strategies as being somewhat manipulative. Now I must tell you, I have just as much integrity as anyone else, but just because I'm willing to put forth an effort that most are not, doesn't make me any less of a good citizen. Like I said before, you can modify these strategies in any way you wish (if it helps your conscience); I'm just giving them to you exactly the way that I used them.

Enough already Joe, what are they? The two remaining strategies are designed to get <u>other students</u> to help you get better grades in school. It's as simple as that. They're pretty straightforward; so let's begin.

Chapter 9: If You Can't Beat'em, Join'em

Objectives:
1. To get the best results from the best students.
2. To learn from your mistakes.
3. To be able to predict your results from the beginning.

Most people in school, be it high school or college, don't care too much for the person who always seems to "ace" every test, project, assignment and course. These "smarty-pants" are the ones who usually ruin the curve for everyone else, raise teacher expectations, and ultimately make our lives miserable. As upsetting as these particular students can sometimes be, they're actually the best thing that can happen to you if you pay attention and play your cards right. I'll explain shortly.

The Myth

Even though we hate to admit it, usually the students who get the best grades in class aren't the smartest, they just work the hardest. Believing that everyone who makes better grades than you is because they're just smarter than you are is a myth. I proved that point when I graduated from college with honors. Given, you do indeed have some Einstein who can get an "A" on a chemistry or calculus exam in their sleep, but believe it or not, there just aren't that many of those types of students out there. The exception would be if you're attending an Ivy League school, and even then, you'd be surprised how many of those students aren't as "smart" as you think they are.

Of course, I didn't know about this "Smart Student Myth" when I was student. But I certainly found out when I became a professor. In my five or so years of teaching two to four courses a semester, with 50 to 125 students per term, I've only had about three, that's right three, students who would be classified as some type of genius. They just loved school, and some even loved studying. They were just made for college. But these students were few and far between.

You still don't believe me? Well, haven't you heard of the National Merit Scholar's Award? This is the award that goes to the nation's best and brightest students. Ask yourself this, how many of them do you think are in each of your classes? Well, I've only taught two in five years, and that includes two different universities (one being ranked #1 nationally in National Merit Scholar recruits).

The reason you don't see that many is because compared to the entire college campus population, the percentage is minuscule (usually less than 1%).

Even when I was a student, I only ran across one National Merit Scholar winner in all of my classes (including my graduate degree). What's my point? Get over the fact that only the "smart students" do well in college, because they don't. Therefore, the students who will consistently do well in your classes won't be the National Merit Scholar winners, but rather the "Blue-collar Joe-Types" who will be busting their hump to be the best.

Remember, an IQ is nothing without an I-Will. Let me show you how you can get these blue-collar types to help you get better grades in college.

If You Can't Beat'em...

The best way to illustrate this strategy is with a personal story. I will summarize the steps for you in a nice little package at the end.

This situation happened to me during a summer term while I was enrolled in a chemistry class. I thoroughly hated that course. I didn't look forward to taking it, but since it was worth four credit hours (with a lab), I knew if I played my cards right and got an "A" out of the course, it could really help me pad my GPA. So I started applying my "tricks" like clockwork.

I had already used Trick #7 (Boring is Better), #8 (the Good Book), #4 (Let Your Fingers Do the Walking), and #5 (The Secret Recipe), and I was ready to get that "A." However, everything changed after my first test, when my professor wrote the grades of our exam on the board. Of course, he didn't write down any names; instead he just wrote down the scores along with the number of students who received those scores. In my best guess at remembering, the grades looked similar to the following (the grades were somewhat inflated because of the nature of the test and course):

$$92 = 1$$
$$87 = 3$$
$$79 = 2$$
$$74 = 6$$
$$63 = 12$$
$$56 \text{ \& below} = 11$$

I must tell you that when I received my grade I was surprised. I didn't get the 92, I got an 87. Surprised really isn't an accurate word describing how I felt; I was highly upset! Why? Because since I was applying my "Tricks" in the classroom (no one else knew them), I usually received the highest grades in all of my classes. Remember, I knew stuff they didn't. So when I received my 87, I was mad and confused. I knew what I knew, but I didn't know what I didn't know.

My professor, who by this time, knew I was a little upset, asked me, "Joe, is there anything wrong?" To that question I nodded yes, and I kindly stood up from my chair and asked, "Who got the 92 on the exam?" This young man in the back of the class raised his hand. And to his response I asked, "Could I see you after class for a minute?" He nodded yes in amazement. Then I sat down and told the professor, "There's no problem sir."

After class, I sought out the young man who outscored me on the exam. I immediately congratulated him on his accomplishments and mentioned to him how hard I had studied myself. Then I asked him the key question, "If you don't mind me asking, how did you study for that exam?" As I shut up to listen to his response, I begin to go through my mental checklist on what I did to study for the test. As he started telling me "his" strategies, I kept scratching things off my list..."I did that, I did that, I did that too." Then all of sudden, guess what? He started mentioning things he did that I didn't do. Before I knew it, he had given me four things that I didn't do. I spare you the boring details.

After our short dialogue, I thanked him profusely for his time and expressed my sincere appreciation for his willingness to share his wisdom. As he made his way to his next class, I quickly wrote down the four things he did that I didn't do, and jetted off to my next class.

To make a long story short, three weeks later, a couple of days before we took our next exam, I used my old study strategies from the first test AND applied the new strategies the top student used to help me study for the second test. A week later when the professor wrote the grades on the board again, take a guess on who had the top score in the class? That's right, yours truly. I got an 88. Hey, that was considered an "A" in chemistry. But more importantly, it was the best score in the class.

So my advice to you, if you can't beat'em, join'em. By the way, that student did not come up to me after class to congratulate me nor to ask me how I had studied for the test. Would I have told him? Sure, because he helped me. But he didn't ask. That's an important lesson in all of this. You can't know everything in life, but you can always know more than the competition. Therefore, if I know what I know, and I know what you know (because you tell me), but you don't know what I know (because you didn't ask me), don't I know more than you? If you have to read that several times do it, because it's worth understanding.

Don't let your pride get in the way because you don't know something. It's like my mother always told me, "The only dumb question is the one you don't ask; because if you don't ask it, you still walk away dumb." That's not too shabby for a person who never went to college.

Quick Trick Action Steps: If You Can't Beat'em Join'em

Steps Summarized:

1. Find out who received the highest grade on the last test (ask the professor if you have to).
2. Find that student and ask how he or she studied for that exam.
3. Make a mental note of things the student did that you didn't do.
4. Write down what the student told you.
5. While studying for the next test, use your strategies and the student's to do better on the next test.
6. If you want overkill, add Trick #10 (Group Therapy) to this strategy.

Chapter 10: Group Therapy

Objectives:

1. To learn how to study smarter.
2. To learn from your mistakes before you make them.
3. To be able to predict your results from the beginning.

Last, but certainly not least, the final "Trick." By now, either you're very excited about what you've read up to this point, and you know this will work for you, or you're saying to yourself, "Man, I could never do what he did." In either case you're right. Henry Ford once said, "Whether a man thinks he can or he can't, he's always right." I can help you change your grades, but I can't control your thinking nor your attitude. That's your job.

Since this strategy is so quick and simple, I will just give you the rationale behind it and a short summary of the action steps. This is another one of those strategies that is easy to do, but hard to follow through. This strategy will take total commitment on your part. Again, I can't teach you that, but if you have a strong enough why (Trick #1), I won't need to. Let's take a look at Trick #10: Group Therapy.

Three or More Is a Crowd

The "Group Therapy" method simply requires you to form a study group with your fellow classmates, and study for the exam the day before you meet with them (as if they were going to give you the test themselves).

The rationale behind this strategy is something you've already heard since grade school, "two heads are better than one." Well if that's true, what about four, six, or eight? Now if you're anything like me, you probably hate study groups. Study groups are usually a justification for putting off studying, reading, and working the way you know you should. If you get in the wrong ones, you can end up wasting time and even worse, bombing the test.

That's why you must form the study group yourself. If you can, try to hand-pick the students you want to participate. The key is for you to stay in control. Be the facilitator. Don't let the conversations get off track and onto soap operas, ball games, and parties. It will be challenging, because you might be the only one who's serious about the purpose of the group. But that's okay. Just be serious.

The second part of this trick, which requires the most commitment on your part, is studying the day before your group meets (as if they were going to test you themselves). This part is what makes this trick so powerful. I must also note that it would probably be best if you didn't tell your group you studied before meeting with them (I'll come back to this later).

Believe me, when your group meets, I would be willing to bet my house that no one would be ready to take that test if it was given on the day of your meeting. All that means is that no one is fully prepared for the exam, except for you. And why should they? that's why most students join study groups. . . to push the studying off on someone else.

So why should you be prepared if others aren't? Five reasons:

1.) To be able to keep the group on track;
2.) To give you a leg up on the competition;
3.) To reinforce the material you learned the night before;
4.) To evaluate how prepared you are for tomorrow's test;
5.) To find out where your blind spots are before they hurt you.

I hope the picture is becoming a little more clear. This method is somewhat similar to Trick #9, except you're stopping trouble before it starts. I've used this method quite a bit, and I can't say I always got an "A" on every test using this strategy, but I can tell you that I always received at least one letter grade better than my group.

This leads into something I mentioned just a minute ago, which was my advice of not telling your group that you studied before the meeting. Why not? I could be totally wrong about this, so you can take this with a grain of salt. The last thing you need on this test is increased competition. If you told them about your strategy, some students might feel insecure about themselves and may not be willing to help you out as much as they could, because they think you're going to outscore them on the test. Like I said, I could be totally wrong on this one. My philosophy on this one was, if you didn't ask, I didn't tell (this was long before Clinton made this phrase popular).

It's up to you. As with all of these strategies, you can modify, add to, or delete anything about them that you don't like. I'm just giving them to you the way I used them. I always tell my students, "It's always better to critique than create." So, make this trick better if you can.

Quick Trick Action Steps: Group Therapy

Steps Summarized:
1. After a test is announced, immediately initiate the formation of a study group.
2. If at all possible, approach those you want to participate.
3. Set up the meeting for the day "before" the exam.
4. Study for the exam the day "before" your group meets.
5. Facilitate the group meeting by making sure the group stays on course.
6. As possible test questions are asked, always try to answer as many of them as you can without referring to your notes.
7. Make a written note of the questions you have a problem answering.

8. After the group session is over, study only the questions you noted in the meeting until you know the answers in your sleep.
9. Quiz yourself one more time before going to bed.

Notes:

The keys to this strategy again is commitment. It will take an effort on your part to study before your group meets. There's a hidden benefit if you do this; the night before the test, you won't have to study the same material you studied the day before (unless you choose to). You only have to study what you didn't know from the study group meeting (the questions you couldn't answer). Remember from the last chapter, you're not only learning what you know, but what they know as well. If they don't learn what you know, your grade on the test should be at least one grade higher than theirs.

Chapter 11: The Big Picture

Well we've reached the end. I know I've thrown a lot of information at you, but hey, you're in college (or at least college-bound), so you can handle it. Here's a quick summary of all 10 of the tricks:

Tricks of the Grade Summary

Part I: Base Building Basics

Quick Trick Action Steps: Why Ask Why?

1. Establish a strong, compelling, personal "WHY" for being in college.
2. Write or type out your "WHY STATEMENT."
3. Test that why statement by asking yourself these three questions:
   a.) Am I willing to do **whatever it takes** to make this a reality?
   b.) Am I willing to **pay the price with blood, sweat, and tears** to graduate?
   c.) Am I willing to **take the garbage** that comes along with the college experience?
4. Ask yourself, did I answer the previous three questions honestly and blamelessly? (If no, find another "why.")
5. Put your why statement in a place that you can read it at least once a week (preferably Mondays).

Quick Trick Action Steps: Determine Your Destination

1. Write down five goals you want to achieve BEFORE you graduate from college.
2. Examine each goal and make sure that each is attainable,

specific, measurable, and has a deadline.

3. Answer the following questions as they pertain to **each one** of the five goals you listed (write out your responses):
   - a.) What will I gain if I achieve this goal?
   - b.) What will it cost me if I don't achieve this goal?
   - c.) Who could help me achieve this goal?
   - d.) What could prevent me from achieving this goal?
   - e.) Who can I get to hold me accountable for my goals (and tell them)?
4. Read your goals at least once a semester.

Quick Trick Action Steps: Break the Curve

1. Do whatever it takes to convince yourself that you can, will, and do deserve an "A" in every course.
2. Find out from the professor or another student if anybody ever earned an "A" in the class before. If so, so can you.
3. Raise your expectations by adopting your own grading system (not your college's).
4. Make "C's" a thing of the past for you.
5. Put forth an effort you can be proud of, and graciously accept whatever grade you get.
6. Ask yourself: do I really <u>expect</u> to get an "A" in this course? If not, start from the top again.

Part II: Teacher Taming Techniques

Quick Trick Action Steps: Let Your Fingers Do the Walking

Steps Summarized:
1. Get a student/campus directory.
2. Get a highlighter (a different color per major).
3. Get a notepad and make a "T" in the

middle of the page. Label "Bad"on the left, and "Good" on the right. (have a blank page for additional notes)

4. Highlight ALL students who have the following characteristics:
   - Senior
   - In your major (or other majors you're having problems with)
   - Have a local number listed (to avoid high telephone bills)
5. Rehearse script (practice, practice, practice).
6. Call each student using a script.

Quick Trick Action Steps: The Secret Recipe

Steps Summarized:
1. Stay after class on the first day.
2. Get a notepad.
3. Ask the instructor for no more than ten (10) minutes of his or her time.
4. Ask the instructor four (4) pre-prepared questions (see script).
5. Write down the instructor's responses to questions 3 and 4 on your notepad.
6. Explain your purpose (why you're asking these questions) to instructor.
7. Thank instructor for his or her time.

Quick Trick Action Rules: The Business of School

1. Try to show up for class everyday even when you don't feel like it.
2. Be on time!
3. Accept personal responsibility for everything that happens to you.
4. Type everything if at all possible.

5. Proofread everything until you're tired of reading it, and then proof it again.
6. Never, never, never argue a grade.
7. Turn ALL assignments in on time.
8. Always do a little more than the average student will do.

Quick Trick Action Rules: Boring is Better

Steps Summarized: 1. Take all of your boring and tough classes over the summer.
2. Don't take more than two courses per summer session (term).
3. Sign up for summer classes taught by full-time professors only (avoid adjuncts).
4. Use Trick #4 (The Recipe) on this professor.

Quick Action Steps: The Good Book

Steps Summarized: 1. Set up an appointment to meet the instructor in his or her office.
2. Ask to see the instructor's syllabus the semester before you enroll.
3. Explain your purpose to instructor (i.e. to be prepared, get quick start, etc.).
4. Ask about assigned reading material (if any, get it).
5. Ask him or her how you can prepare for the class.
6. Quickly scan the syllabus and ask questions if you have any.
7. Thank instructor for his or her time.

Part III: Street-Smart Study Strategies

Quick Trick Action Steps: If You Can't Beat'em Join'em

Steps Summarized:
1. Find out who received the highest grade on the last test (ask the professor if you have to).
2. Find that student and ask how he or she studied for that exam.
3. Make a mental note of things you didn't do that the student did.
4. Write down what the student told you.
5. While studying for the next test, use your strategies and the student's to do better on the next test.
6. If you want overkill, add Trick #10 (Group Therapy) to this strategy.

Quick Trick Action Steps: Group Therapy

Steps Summarized:
1. After a test is announced, immediately initiate the formation of a study group.
2. Set up the meeting for the day before the exam.
3. Study for the exam the day before your group meets.
4. Facilitate the group meeting by making sure the group stays on course.
5. As possible test questions are asked, always try to answer as many as you can without referring to your notes.
6. Make note of the questions you have a problem answering.
7. After the group session is over, study only the questions you noted in the meeting until you know the answers.
8. Quiz yourself one more time before going to bed.

To get the most out of this book, I would advise you to re-read Tricks #1-3. They're the most important components of this book. Without them as a foundation, your house will be blown away by the even the slightest breeze. Internalize them and utilize them.

As a "successful" college graduate and professor, I'm more convinced than ever that higher education, like life, is a game. Those who know the rules win, and those who don't know end up feeling frustrated and cheated.

Although we've focused on how to achieve better grades in college, don't lose sight of the big picture. I always tell my students, no matter how much they refuse to believe it, most professors understand what students go through. There isn't a professor around who has never been a student; who's never had to study; who's never had to turn in assignments on time; who's never had to take boring courses and tough professors.

However, I also ask my students, how many of them have ever been a professor? Until this day, no student has ever said he or she has. That means, contrary to popular belief, professors understand you much better than you understand them. And hopefully, I've helped you to understand them a little better than you did before.

I personally believe teaching is one of the most rewarding and most frustrating jobs there is. As a professor, we have to make decisions that can effect and direct a student's future. Very few students don't realize how tough it is for professors to actually fail a student they know has the potential, but just isn't utilizing it. Few students don't know how tough it is to believe in students more than they believe in themselves. And even fewer students don't know how tough if it is trying to rebuild a student's confidence when he or she attaches their self-esteem to something as insignificant as a grade.

Although I have given you the tools you need to crack this system we call college, I want you to remember something else my mother told me. She said, "You're just as good as anyone else. No one is better than you, but remember, you're not better than anyone else either." These words help me to stay humble and not forget where I came from.

As a child growing up in the ghettos of Miami, I realize now that attending college was not a right, but a privilege. Greater people before us have paid the price for us to have the opportunity to pursue our dreams. Attending college doesn't make you better or smarter than those who aren't. In the big picture, college is just a means to an end, not the end itself. It's an opportunity that creates more opportunities, but it's not the ONLY opportunity.

So as you get a step closer to your goals, your dreams, and your graduation date, keep these words of wisdom in mind, "Learning is a lifelong process, it shouldn't stop until you do. Never stop learning!"

The recurring theme in this entire book is the fact that if you are willing to do the opposite of what most are willing to do, you will get better results. It's been repeated several times for a reason....to make sure it becomes fixated in you mind. To that end, I leave you with this poem that I dedicate to you entitled, "Not Like Most." Read it, internalize it, and live it. God bless!

<u>Not Like Most</u>

While most have decided to become part of the problem,
we have chosen to be part of the solution;
While most have questioned "Why?"
we have dared to ask "Why Not?"
While most have accepted defeat,
we have accepted the challenge to compete;
While most have focused on the obstacles,
we have focused on the openings;
While most have been overwhelmed by difficulties,
we have transformed them into opportunities;
While most have given up,
we have certainly not given in;

While most have resolved to talk,
we have resolved to take action;
While most have lost all hope,
we have remained hopeful;
While most are discouraged by the output,
we are encouraged by the possible outcome;
While most have forgotten from whence they came,
we haven't forgotten who brought us this far;
And while most wish they were like us,
we thank God we're not like most.

Joe A. Martin, Jr.

Live with purpose, passion, and power!

Note to the Reader:

If you would like to receive on-going support throughout your college journey, please come visit us at RealWorld University:

www.rwuniversity.com

RWU is the only university in the country where **success** is the **only** major! We teach you the things most colleges won't.

In addition to helping you improve your GPA, RWU helps you face some of the toughest challenges associated with the college experience (as identified by college students from all across the country). At RealWorld University, our job is to find the answers, and your job is to apply them. Visit us today!

NOTES

NOTES

NOTES

NOTES

NOTES

NOTES